Florida Seafood Cookery

by Lowis Carlton

PUBLISHING CO.
4747 TWENTY-EIGHTH STREET NORTH
ST. PETERSBURG, FLORIDA 33714

International Standard Book No.: 0-8200-0809-5

Library of Congress Catalog Card Number 91-70788

Photo Credits: Photos on pages 6, 57, 67 provided courtesy of Florida News Bureau, Dept. of Commerce. Photo on page 86 provided courtesy of the American Dairy Association.

Color Photo Credits: Color photo page 49 provided courtesy of National Macaroni Institute. Author's photo by Claud Carlton. All other color photos (including cover photo) provided courtesy of Florida Department of Natural Resources, Bureau of Seafood Marketing.

Cover: Baked Florida Mullet with Hot 'N Sassy Tartar Sauce; recipe page 41.

Printed in the United States of America

Contents

About the Author

Lowis Carlton is the author of *Famous Florida Recipes* and has written for a variety of national publications. She was graduated Magna Cum Laude from the University of Miami with a B.A. and M.A. in English, and was named to Phi Kappa Phi for high achievements. She also holds a B.S. in Home Economics from Florida International University, where she concentrated on work with the chefs in the school's highly rated hotel school.

While serving as Food Editor for the *Miami Herald*, Lowis won the Vespa Award in competition with all newspapers nationwide. She served as a judge for the Pillsbury Bake-Off, and has traveled extensively in Europe, studying food customs.

Lowis was Gourmet Editor for *Palm Beach Life* magazine for many years, also a columnist for the Florida Department of Agriculture, writing about Florida products for 200 newspapers throughout the U.S.

After residing in Miami for many years, Lowis and husband Claud recently moved to Palm City, Florida, where they have a home beside a lake and now dispense bushels of bird feed for a multitude of wild birds.

Though husband Claud is semi-retired, Lowis maintains a full schedule developing and testing recipes, participating in church work, and doing research for a Florida novel. Hobbies for the Carltons are traveling all over the world, playing bridge, fishing, and enjoying the recipes contained in this book.

Foreword

Fish is the food of choice in today's world — low in calories and high in nutrition. How nice to know that something so good to eat is so good for you! It's versatile, too. You can dress it up for elegant party fare, or dress it down for simple but delicious family fare.

Testing the recipes and writing this book became a labor of love for this home economist; but there was a problem. With so many varieties of food from sea and stream available in our Sunshine State, literally hundreds of them, space limitations prevented my using them all. I had to choose the best known, most popular fish and seafood, including a variety of appetizers, soups, salads and main dishes. If your favorite local fish did not make the list, please forgive. Maybe next time!

I hope this cookbook will stimulate your interest, that you will continue enjoying familiar recipes (such as fried shrimp) — but also have fun trying new ones (such as Peruvian seviche). When you must whip up a meal in minutes, the chapter on "can-venient" cooking should help. By all means, use the chapter on outdoor cooking and entertain Florida style, day or night. You will discover how marvelous food from the deep can taste grilled over charcoal or smoked over mesquite or applewood.

Sincere thanks go to the Florida Department of Natural Resources, Bureau of Seafood Marketing — especially Marilyn Rose and Marie W. Holmes — for photographs and up-to-the-minute statistical information on nutrition. Also, to the American Dairy Association and Florida News Bureau for photographs.

Now please turn the page and enter the exciting world of fish cookery. Truly, here is food you can enjoy — to your heart's delight!

Lowis Carlton

Bounty from the sea includes shrimp, oysters, stone crab, blue crab, mullet, redfish and pompano.

How to Cook Fish

Now you have caught a fish, or brought one home from the market. The big question is "How should it be cooked?" The answer is "Any way you like — and you have a tremendous variety of methods and recipes to choose from." In this book you will find Florida's favorite ways to cook fish.

There is one unfailing rule you must observe — never overcook fish! Or any other seafood, either. Cooked at too high a temperature for too long, the most juicy, delectable fish will turn tough and dry.

To determine cooking time, use the following rule: Allow 10 minutes of cooking time for each inch of thickness. Place the fish or fillet on a flat surface and measure the thickest point, then time your cooking accordingly.

How do you know when fish is done? Because cooking time is usually short, it may be difficult at first to know when fish is done, but not overcooked. Raw fish flesh has a watery, translucent look, and the juices look watery, too. During cooking, the flesh will turn opaque and whitish in color, and the juices will turn milky colored. At this point, the fish will flake when tested with a fork.

Here's a friendly warning. When first you cook fish, you may be disappointed. Because cooking time is short, you may find it difficult to get perfect results. Don't be discouraged! Practice... repeat the recipe... check the timing with your cooking equipment and the one particular recipe. You will become an expert, but it may take a little practice to become perfect. You can be sure that the compliments you will get will be well worth the effort!

After a few sessions, you will know — by testing for texture and color — just how long to cook your fish to get it just the way you want it.

Among the cooking methods, pan-frying, broiling and baking are the most popular. Other methods are barbecuing, deep-frying, microwaving, oven-frying, poaching and steaming.

If you cook the fish simply, why not make a superb sauce that will turn it into a gourmet delight? The chapter on sauces will give you good suggestions.

Some of the finest recipes in the Florida Keys and the Bahamas are based on rich fish stock. It's easy to make and really intensifies the flavor in fish dishes. You can make an excellent fish stock from the head and bones of lean fish such as snapper. Rinse under cold running water and place in a pot with carrots, onions, celery and your favorite herbs (such as peppercorns, bay leaf and allspice). Cover with water, bring to a boil and simmer 20 to 30 minutes. Skim and strain the liquid, and discard the bones. Use at once, or freeze in ice cube trays to use in the future.

Baking

For fillets or steaks up to 1½ inches thick, and for whole or stuffed fish.

Whatever the size, shape or kind of fish you choose, adding to the pan a half-cup of basting sauce such as chicken broth or dry white wine insures good flavor. Or, use water with herbs added, such as onion, parsley, dried basil, thyme or marjoram. For simple baking, you might add a rich sauce such as Hollandaise.

To bake a fish, wash and pat dry with paper towels. Lightly oil a baking pan and place it in the oven to preheat, at a temperature from 375°F to 425°F, depending on your recipe. Dust the fish with seasoned flour and lightly coat it with vegetable oil or basting sauce. (High temperatures cook quickly and seal juices inside.)

Place fish in the pan in a single layer and bake uncovered, using the rule of 10 minutes cooking time for each inch of fish thickness. Turn the fish once; test for doneness three-quarters of the way through the cooking time. (Allow 50% more time for a whole stuffed fish than for fillets.)

Carefully remove fish to a warm platter and pour pan juices over, or serve with a chosen sauce.

Barbecuing

For fillets, steaks, small whole fish, skewered chunks or large, whole fish.

Moderately fat fish such as trout, bluefish and mackerel take superb flavor from the smoke of the barbecue — much better than more delicate fish such as flounder.

To make it easy to barbecue fish, it will pay you to invest in a hinged long-handled wire basket. Without this, tender fish is likely to fall apart when you try to turn it or remove it from the grill.

Grease the grill; grease the wire basket. Florida's warm climate makes it advisable to keep your fish refrigerated until you are ready to cook it. If you are using a charcoal grill, start the fire 30 minutes or more ahead of time and let the charcoal burn down to glowing coals. All fish must be basted with butter or a marinade while cooking, to prevent it from drying out. If a marinade is used, pour it over the fish and refrigerate from 30 minutes to two hours, as the recipe states.

For honest Florida flavor, the juice of ripe Florida grapefruit makes a very good marinade.

For equipment, you may use a portable charcoal or gas grill, smoke cooker, or small hibachi. Be sure to read the instruction sheet or recipe book for the unit.

For more information and recipes using various equipment, see the chapter on Outdoor Cooking.

Broiling

For fillets and steaks ½ to 1½ inches thick (thicker is better), and split, whole fish.

The thickness of fish determines how far below the broiler unit it should be: from two inches for thin fillets to about five inches for thicker fish. (It's best to experiment with your own broiler and favorite fish to find exactly the correct distance for perfect results.)

Today, with so many people watching their weight, broiling is a favorite, non-greasy way to cook fish.

For split fish, leave the skin on; do the same with fillets. Plan to use a tasty marinade or basting sauce, flavored with lemon, lime, wine or teriyaki. If you use a marinade, wipe fish with a damp cloth and cut it into serving size pieces. Place in a glass or other non-metal dish, cover with marinade and refrigerate 30 minutes or more. Drain well before broiling.

If you prefer to coat the fish, rub fish with vegetable oil or melted butter, and then roll it in cornmeal, wheat germ or crushed cereal. To keep lean fish from drying out, baste it with plenty of vegetable oil or melted butter.

To broil fish, oil the broiler rack and preheat. Coat the fish if you plan to baste with melted butter or oil while broiling. When using a marinade, place the fish on oiled rack and baste once or twice during broiling. (Of course, you need a pan or foil below to catch drippings.) Depending upon the thickness of the fish, broil somewhere between two and five inches from the heat.

Broil until the fish browns lightly and test it with a fork; it should flake easily and look opaque. Thin pieces need not be turned. Pieces thicker than three-quarters of an inch thick should be turned once.

Remember, don't overcook! And do practice until you get the exact cooking time and distance from heat that gives you a perfect dish.

Deep Frying

For fillets, steaks, nuggets, fish sticks, and small whole fish (cleaned and scaled).

This is probably the most expensive way to cook fish, and for some people it is also the most difficult. That's because the temperature of the cooking oil must be sufficiently high to cook the fish quickly, and the high temperature must be maintained. This means that large amounts of cold fish must not be added to the oil, because the temperature will be reduced, resulting in greasy fish.

Microwaving

For defrosting and/or cooking fillets, steaks, whole fish or stuffed fish.

Many folks like to microwave their fish. For thawing frozen fish, it is unrivaled. But for cooking fish, in my opinion, other methods are better. Why? First, the chief advantage in microwaving is speed. It cooks food in a hurry. But when you fry, broil or barbecue fish, it cooks just as quickly, and looks far more appetizing because the fish cooks to a golden brown. Microwaved fish remains colorless and needs additional broiling or baking to take on color, unless a sauce is added.

Second, fish cooks quickly at high temperatures, remaining tender and moist. Since delicate fish flesh must never be overcooked, lest it become tough and dry, and because microwaving is so very fast, timing becomes critical. An extra 30 to 60 seconds can be disastrous. This makes it difficult to turn out perfectly cooked fish.

As for cooking time, it is important to realize that microwaved fish must be allowed to stand for several minutes, covered, after cooking. This means that microwaved fish may actually require more total cooking time than more conventional methods.

Difference in power and operating features of various ovens makes it difficult to generalize in microwave recipes. For example, on some ovens "High" is the 100% power setting, while "Medium" indicates 70%. On other ovens, numbered settings correspond to the percent of power; for instance, 5 might correspond to 50%, 1 to 10%, et cetera.

Best results are obtained if you consult the operating manual for your particular type of oven, experiment and make notes for future use. With fish, always undercook and test with a fork several times toward the end of the cooking time.

Defrosting Fish with the Microwave

Unwrap frozen fish or leave it in the wrapping, as you wish, and place it in a baking dish or roasting pan to catch the juices. Turn thicker parts around to the outside edges, thinner parts toward the center. Use the "Defrost" setting.

Type	Weight	Cooking Time*	Standing Time
Fish fillets	1 lb.	5 to 8 min.	5-10 min. (per recipe)
Fish steaks	1 lb.	4 to 7 min.	5-10 min. (per recipe)
Whole Fish	1½ to 2 lbs.	18 to 25 min.	5-10 min. (per recipe)

*Note: These are estimated times, and may vary with different brands of ovens. For exact defrosting times, check the instruction manual for your oven.

How to Cook Fish with the Microwave

Always completely defrost fish or seafood before microwaving, to prevent overcooking. Follow the cooking time recommended in your oven manual and cook only until fish is opaque, or shellfish turns from pink to red and begins to feel firm. Brush with melted butter or lemon juice.

Arrange fish so that thicker parts are around the edges of the oven, with thinner parts turned toward the center. When microwaving coated, sauced fish, cook uncovered or lightly covered with waxed paper. Start checking for doneness at the minimum cooking time (such as 4 minutes with a 4- to 7-minute cooking time), using a fork to test for flakiness.

Use your microwave cookbook to get times required for cooking and for standing, covered, after cooking and before serving. For more recipes, invest in a microwave cookbook containing kitchen-tested recipes.

Oven Frying

For fish fillets a half-inch thick or more, small whole fish (cleaned and scaled) or fish steaks.

Preheat oven to 500°F. Using a shallow baking pan, add ⅛ inch or more of vegetable oil (or half melted butter and half vegetable oil), and preheat. Dip serving-size pieces of fish into melted butter or margarine and place them in the pan in a single layer.

Follow the rule of 10 minutes of cooking time for each one inch of thickness at the fish's thickest part. Cook about five minutes on each side, uncovered, until fish flakes easily with a fork.

Many different batters may be used, such as dipping each piece into egg beaten lightly with milk, then rolling in cracker crumbs or fine dry bread crumbs mixed with grated Parmesan cheese or ground pecans.

Pan Frying

For fillets or steaks.

Dry fish thoroughly. If frozen, thaw in refrigerator just before cooking. Prepare a coating. Dip fish in flour, then in egg beaten with a little water, then in crumbs (bread or cracker crumbs, or crushed cereal). Let stand 5 minutes, then sprinkle with salt and pepper. (Use thawed fish immediately; do not refreeze.)

Pour vegetable oil into skillet to ⅛-inch depth; heat to hot but not smoking. Place fish pieces side by side in a single layer. Brown fish on one side, then carefully turn to brown other side. Allow 10 minutes total cooking time for each inch of the fish's thickness. (Other ideas for coatings: cornmeal, ground almonds or walnuts.)

Poaching

For fillets, steaks, small whole fish or whole, stuffed fish.

Important! The savory liquid used in poaching should simmer; it should *never* come to a boil! It may be salted water, water flavored with herbs and spices, white wine, or other liquid. Because the poaching liquid is deliciously flavored, after the fish is removed to a plate, the liquid may be reduced and thickened to create a gourmet-quality sauce for the hot fish. The liquid may also be frozen and used later as a base for chowder.

Usually, low-fat fish are best suited to poaching, although every rule is made to be broken, and a mild-tasting fatty fish such as salmon is delicious poached and served in its own sauce as a hot entree.

Because fish is so tender, it can easily fall apart and be tricky to handle. If poaching appeals to you, it would be wise to invest in a long, oval pan made for poaching fish. Lacking that pan, which has a lift-out rack, you may opt to wrap cheesecloth around the fish to help it hold its shape and make it easy for you to lift it from the pan. Just be sure you leave both ends of the cloth outside, for lifting, and keep the ends of the cheesecloth away from the stove burner!

Poached fish is tasty and because it cooks without added fat, it is a great favorite with dieters and cholesterol-conscious diners. If you like, poached fish may be browned under the broiler. The sauces you serve with crabmeat are also delicious with poached fish.

To poach fillets or steaks, place serving-size pieces in a skillet and cover them with boiling water. Season with six whole peppercorns, a bay leaf, and two teaspoons lemon juice. Simmer (don't boil) about 10 minutes or until tender. Strain the stock, cook until reduced, and pour over the hot fish. See Sauces chapter for ideas.

Steaming

For non-oily, small, whole fish, such as yellowtail or dolphin. (Thick, firm-fleshed fillets of other fish may also be steamed, but some other methods may be preferable.)

You may use a fish steamer, an oriental steamer in a wok, or place a rack in a roasting pan or electric skillet. Whichever method you use, plan to place a dish or piece of foil under the fish so none of the wonderful juices will be lost.

Immediately after purchasing fish, rinse with cold water, pat dry with paper towels and store in a glass container, lightly covered, in the coldest part of the refrigerator. Fully frozen fish steaks may be steamed while still frozen.

With a whole fish, do not remove the head. Remove any scales or fins, closely trim gills and rinse fish well under cold running water. Cut diagonal slashes ¼ to ½ inch deep across the body, one inch apart, starting one inch below the head and going to two inches short of the tail. Repeat on the other side.

Use one tablespoon salt for each two quarts of water. (Stock or flavored broth may also be used.) Bring liquid to a boil. Lightly oil the steamer rack and line with lettuce or foil. Place fish on rack, cover and steam for 10 minutes per inch of thickness of the fish, or until the fish tests done.

How to tell when fish is done? Uncooked, the flesh is translucent; steaming will turn it opaque or milky looking. To test, use two forks and gently pull away the flesh at a center point of the fish. You may wish to cut a small slit in the center with a sharp knife and pull it apart to check, instead. Beware of overcooking; the minute the fish turns opaque, it is ready to be removed from the heat.

Steamed fish may be served with a sauce such as Browned Butter or Hollandaise. Because steaming leaves fish white, plan to add a colorful garnish of cherry tomatoes, watercress, parsley, slices of avocado or radish roses.

Nutritional Fish Facts

Health-conscious Americans are choosing more low-fat foods because the calorie count is also frequently low, which helps keep them slim. According to many medical researchers, a low-fat diet can also cut the risk of heart disease and certain cancers. Because fish and seafood are low-fat and low-calorie, they have become enormously popular throughout the country. Floridians are especially blessed, because they have a wealth of food from sea and stream to choose from, much of it fresh from waters in and around the state.

Fish is an integral part of every expert's ideal, healthful diet. While the role of cholesterol in the diet is still highly controversial, most nutrition experts now consider that a healthful diet should contain about two-thirds plant foods (fruits, vegetables, legumes and grains) and one-third animal foods (meat, poultry, fish and dairy products). This proportion may be further broken down, to get the following recommendation:

- 30% of daily calories from fat foods, but no more than 10% from saturated fats (including butter, milk, cheese, meat, cream, coconut oil).

- 70% of daily calories from non-fat plant foods, and no more than 300 milligrams of cholesterol each day.

Fish is especially beneficial when it is used to replace meats and dairy products that are high in saturated fats.

Questions About Nutrition

Q. Why are fish and seafood so healthful?

A. They are high in protein, low in cholesterol, fat, sodium and calories. They are rich in vitamins and easy to digest.

Q. Would you give us details, and state which fish is lowest in cholesterol?

A. The charts on pages 19 and 20 are the official listing from the U.S. Department of Commerce's *USDA Handbook Eight (1987) Composition of Foods: Finfish and Shellfish.* You'll note that monkfish, bluefin tuna, grouper and red snapper lead the low-cholesterol list, but many others are not far behind. It's important to remember that numbers on the chart are only approximations. Figures can vary, depending on location, season, age of fish, spawning, and which part of the fish is tested.

Q. So, how do we use the chart?

A. Check which types of fish and seafood are high and which are low sources, then plan menus which include less of the high-content types and more of the low-content types. Keep in mind that theses figures are approximations, and so may vary from one chart to the next.

Lean fish species are considered to be those with a fat content from 0.5 percent to not more than 5 percent, with oil concentrated in the liver. Due to this low oil content, you may freeze these fish for up to six months, and the very leanest up to one year.

Fat (or oily) fish species are those with oil content of more than 5 percent. Oil is distributed throughout the flesh of the fish, causing the flesh color to be darker than that of lean fish. The exact percentage of oil varies, depending on species, season, even the depth of the water where the fish was taken. Limit freezer time for oily fish to three months.

Q. How do other foods compare with fish and seafood in cholesterol content?

A. Here are a few examples which show the approximate amount of cholesterol for various foods. (For complete information, consult a nutritional guidebook.) These figures were supplied by the Florida Department of Natural Resources, Bureau of Seafood Marketing:

Food	Serving Size	Cholesterol
Ground beef, extra lean	3½ ounces	70 mg.
Pork loin, extra lean	3½ ounces	65 "
Chicken, light meat, no skin	3½ ounces	60 "
Peanut butter and other legumes	3½ ounces	0 "
Cheddar cheese	2 ounces	60 "
Butter	1 tablespoon	30 "
Margarine	1 tablespoon	0 "
Egg yolk	large egg	213 "
Egg white	large egg	0 "

Q. Is it true that shrimp and lobster are higher in cholesterol than other foods?

A. Somewhat higher, yes. But one serving of 3.5 ounces of shrimp has less than the amount of cholesterol in one medium egg. So you can eat 1⅓ servings of shrimp and it would equal no more than one egg. Also, these seafoods are low in calories and saturated fat, which is a real plus.

Q. Does cooking affect the cholesterol content in fish and other seafood?

A. No, not unless you combine them with egg yolks, butter, cream or cheese.

Q. I've heard that raw clams and oysters can make you sick if they come from contaminated waters. True?

A. Yes, it's true. Shellfish, such as oysters, clams and mussels are filter feeders, and tend to concentrate any toxins or bacteria that may be present in the water. To protect your safety, the Department of Natural Resources and other agencies monitor waters from which shellfish are taken, and these must be approved.

A word of caution: if you go out to catch your own seafood, first be sure to check with your local Health Department or Florida Marine Patrol office to be sure the waters are free of pollution. While most oysters are safe to eat raw, to avoid problems with bacteria experts now recommend that they be thoroughly cooked, especially by kidney patients, diabetics, AIDS patients and people regularly taking antacids. Also, wash well all knives and utensils that raw oysters contact.

Q. Any other suggestions?

A. Keep your hands clean and handle fish as little as possible. Keep all fish and seafood well chilled until cooking or serving time; this is especially important in Florida's warm climate. *Never* let food stand around on a picnic table for hours. Keep it in the ice box.

Buy your fish really fresh from a reputable market, on the day that you will use it. Some fine fish markets even pack your fish in crushed ice for you, to keep it chilled during the ride home!

Q. What can you tell me about Omega-3?

A. Omega-3 is a fatty acid found in fish oils which, according to American Chemical Society tests, protects beneficial aspects of cholesterol and may reduce high blood pressure. Reportedly, Omega-3 causes excess sodium to be excreted, which lowers blood pressure and helps keep good electrolyte balance in the body.

Q. Where is it found?

A. All fish and seafood contain some Omega-3, but oily (fatty) fish have the most. According to the University of Florida Seafood Nutrient experts, the following kinds of fish contain more than one gram of Omega-3 per 100 grams edible uncooked portion: Atlantic mackerel, 1.80; Atlantic herring, 1.31; Spanish mackerel, 1.07; bluefish, 0.66; striped mullet, 0.63; swordfish, 0.62; rainbow trout, 0.57; Spanish sardine, 0.54; pompano, 0.50. Among shellfish, blue crab has 0.41 grams Omega-3 per 100 gram serving; Eastern oyster, 0.38; spiny lobster, 0.30; shrimp, 0.32.

Q. So a healthy diet should contain Omega-3?

A. Absolutely! Two or three servings a week of fish listed above is recommended, and not just for health's sake. It's really delicious! ❧

LEAN FISH	Calories (per 100g)	Protein (g/100g)	Fat (g/100g)	Cholesterol (mg/100g)	Sodium (mg/100g)	Iron (mg/100g)
Catfish	116	18.18	4.26	58	63	0.97
Dolphin	85	18.50	0.70	73	88	1.13
Flounder	91	18.84	1.19	48	81	0.36
Grouper	92	19.38	1.02	37	53	0.89
Monkfish	76	14.48	1.52	25	18	0.32
Ocean Perch	94	18.62	1.63	42	75	0.92
Sea Trout	104	16.74	3.61	83	58	0.27
Shark	130	20.98	4.51	51	79	0.84
Snapper, Red	100	20.51	1.34	37	64	0.18
Swordfish	121	19.80	4.01	39	90	0.81
Tilefish	96	17.50	2.31	n/a	53	0.25
Whiting	90	18.31	1.31	67	72	0.34

FAT (or Oily) FISH	Calories (per 100g)	Protein (g/100g)	Fat (g/100g)	Cholesterol (mg/100g)	Sodium (mg/100g)	Iron (mg/100g)
Bluefish	124	20.04	4.24	59	60	0.48
Eel	184	18.44	11.66	126	51	0.51
Mullet	117	19.35	3.79	49	65	1.02
Pompano	164	18.48	9.47	50	65	0.60
Salmon, Pink	116	19.94	3.45	52	67	0.77
Spanish Mackerel	139	19.29	6.30	76	59	0.44
Tuna, bluefin	144	23.33	4.90	38	39	1.02
SHELLFISH						
Blue Crab	87	18.06	1.08	78	3	0.74
Clams	74	12.77	0.97	34	56	13.98
Lobster, Spiny	112	20.60	1.51	70	2	1.22
Mussels	86	11.90	2.24	28	286	3.95
Oysters, Gulf	69	7.06	2.47	55	112	6.70
Scallops	88	16.78	0.76	33	161	0.29
Shrimp	106	20.31	1.73	152	148	2.41

Florida Fish Recipes

Catfish

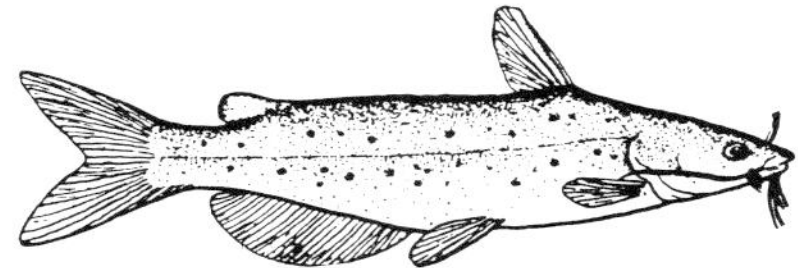

Millions of catfish are consumed each year, throughout the southern and central states, caught by sport fishermen as well as by commercial boats, and raised on increasingly popular catfish farms. Once, catfish was popular only below the Mason-Dixon line, but now northern restaurants and supermarkets are featuring this gastronomic delight. Some 28 varieties of catfish, salt and freshwater, are found in the United States.

The mild-flavored white meat is delectable in this lean fish. The thick, slippery skin must be removed before the fish is cut into fillets or steaks, and should be handled with care to avoid the sharp, spiny rays on the fins.

In Florida, the 730-square mile Lake Okeechobee — the name means "big water" — is Florida's prime source for freshwater catfish. In the tiny towns clustered around the big lake, catfish tops the menu in dozens of small restaurants. Old-timers like catfish best fried, either whole or in fillets, served with hot little hush puppies and plenty of hot grits. But catfish is also great grilled whole, broiled, stuffed and sautéed, stir-fried, or simmered in gumbos.

Use catfish as an excellent substitute in recipes calling for sole, flounder, or haddock. Rewrap fresh fish, refrigerate, and cook within two days.

Here is the prize winner in the 1978 National Farm-Raised Catfish Cooking Contest. It's guaranteed to win raves!

Stuffed Farm-Raised Catfish Almondine

8 small, pan-dressed, farm-raised catfish
½ cup white wine
1 Tbsp. onion, chopped
½ tsp. salt
¼ tsp. pepper
10 medium, cooked shrimp, chopped
1 6-oz. can crabmeat, well drained
¾ cup butter or margarine
1 4-oz. package sliced almonds
1 Tbsp. lemon or lime juice
cherry tomatoes
parsley and lemon wedges

Thaw catfish if frozen, in refrigerator. Clean thoroughly and dry with paper towels. Combine wine, onion, salt, pepper, shrimp and crabmeat; marinate for 30 minutes. Drain and save liquid. If the cavity of the fish is small, enlarge it by cutting a small pocket along the backbone. Stuff each fish with the shrimp and crabmeat mixture. Sprinkle fish with salt. Fry in margarine until browned on each side and fish is done; it should flake easily when tested with a fork. Remove fish from pan to a warm platter. Add almonds, lemon juice and reserved marinade to frying pan; cook until almonds are lightly browned. Spread sauce over catfish and garnish with tomatoes, parsley and lemon wedges. **Serves 4.**

Creamy Baked Catfish Fillets

1½ pounds catfish fillets
½ cup mayonnaise
1 cup dairy sour cream
1½ tsp. Beau Monde seasoning
⅛ tsp. mild mustard
⅛ tsp. ground ginger
¼ tsp. salad herbs
⅛ tsp. white pepper
paprika

Thaw fish if frozen. Place fillets in well-greased baking pan. Mix together mayonnaise, sour cream, Beau Monde, mustard, ginger and pepper. Crush herbs and mix into sour cream mixture. Spread over fish. Sprinkle with paprika. Bake in preheated 350°F oven for about 30 minutes, or until fish flakes easily and the sauce is bubbling. Serve at once, if desired, with piping hot rice pilaf. (You may also run the fish under the broiler for a minute or two until lightly browned.) **Serves 3 to 4.**

Catfish in Potato Jackets

4 small catfish, cleaned and skinned
½ tsp. salt
⅛ tsp. pepper
1 egg
1 Tbsp. water
1 cup instant mashed potatoes
1 envelope onion salad dressing mix
½ tsp. paprika
vegetable oil or margarine

Thaw fish if frozen. Wipe fish with damp cloth. Rub inside and out with salt and pepper. In one bowl, mix egg with water. In another bowl, combine potato flakes and dressing mix with paprika. Place enough oil in frying pan to cover bottom; heat oil until it is hot but not smoking. Dip each piece of fish in egg mixture, then into potato mixture. Repeat. Cook fish in hot oil for 4 to 5 minutes, until it is browned on one side; turn fish and repeat with other side. When done, the fish should be golden brown and easy to flake with a fork. Serve hot with french fries and a crisp green salad — and hushpuppies, of course! **Serves 4.**

Catfish Soup-Stew, Yankee Style

1 pound catfish fillets
1½ cups sliced carrots
1 cup water
1 10½-oz. can condensed cream of potato soup
1 9-oz. package frozen cut green beans, thawed
1 10-oz. can tomatoes
1 cup undiluted evaporated milk
1½ tsp. onion salt
¼ tsp. leaf thyme
oyster crackers

Thaw fish if frozen; cut into 1-inch pieces. Combine carrots and water in saucepan. Cover and simmer 15 minutes or until carrots are almost tender. Stir in potato soup, green beans, tomatoes, milk, salt, thyme; heat until hot and bubbly. Add fish; cover and cook about 10 minutes or until fish flakes easily and beans are tender. Serve with a bowl of oyster crackers. **Serves 4.**

Florida Catfish with Noodles

8 oz. wide egg noodles
2 pounds catfish fillets
½ cup butter or margarine
½ cup chopped pecans
2 Tbsp. onion, finely chopped
½ tsp. salt
¼ tsp. pepper
⅛ tsp. nutmeg
1½ Tbsp. lime juice
lime wedges
canned pimiento
toasted pecan halves

Cook noodles as shown on the package; drain and turn into oiled, 2-quart, shallow baking dish. Arrange fish fillets over noodles. Combine butter, chopped pecans, onion, salt, pepper and nutmeg. Cook over low heat, stirring now and then, until mixture comes to a boil. Add lime juice and mix. Pour over fish fillets. Bake in preheated 375°F oven for 35 minutes, or until fish flakes easily. Garnish with lime wedges, pimiento, and pecan halves. **Serves 6.**

Baked Catfish Espagne

1 Tbsp. cooking oil
1 cup onion, thinly sliced
1½ pounds catfish fillets
1½ tsp. salt
¼ tsp. pepper
¼ tsp. nutmeg
⅛ tsp. cayenne
2 large tomatoes, sliced
2 Tbsp. chopped chives
1 3-oz. can sliced broiled mushrooms
1 Tbsp. white wine
½ tsp. brown gravy sauce
½ cup buttered bread crumbs

Place oil in a shallow baking dish large enough to hold fish in a single layer. Spread evenly with sliced onion. Lay fish over onion. Sprinkle fish with salt, pepper, nutmeg, and cayenne blended together. Top with sliced tomatoes, sprinkle with chives. Combine contents of can of mushrooms, wine and bottled brown gravy sauce; pour over fish. Bake in preheated 400°F oven for 15 minutes, then top with buttered crumbs. Continue baking until crumbs are browned and the fish is done, about 15 minutes more. **Serves 4.**

Dolphin

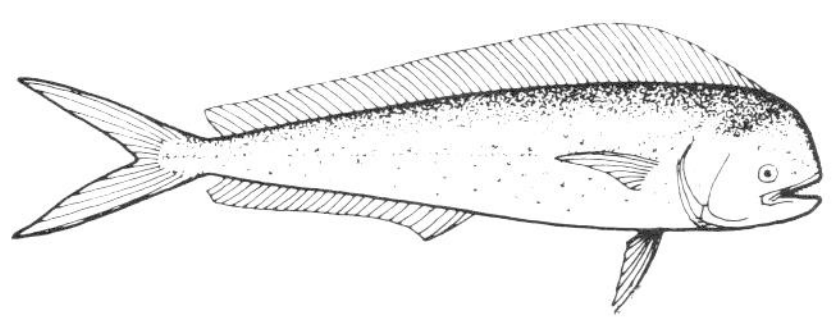

The dolphin is a brilliant green and golden color when hooked, but it soon fades to gray when out of the water. It is called *mahimahi* in Hawaii, but is usually called dolphin in Florida. (These are sports fish, weighing from two to 50 pounds, and are not the big, lovable fellows — mammals who are members of the porpoise family — who jump and cavort in places like Sea World.)

Dolphin thrive in all tropical and subtropical seas, from North Carolina to Florida and throughout the Caribbean to Brazil. To protect the delectable flavor, wise fishermen cut the tail off and drain the fish immediately after it is caught. By having the fish bleed before it is stored on ice, the flavor is noticeably better. Dolphin meat is unique, with its large sweet-tasting flakes. The roe of the female is superb. It is a terrifically versatile fish which can be baked, braised, grilled, sautéed, broiled, or mixed into a chowder.

At elegant Palm Beach dinner parties, dolphin is a favorite hors d'oeuvre — skinned, cut into cubes and bathed in a lime juice marinade, then broiled with garlic butter, either in the oven or over charcoal on the grill.

Dolphin can be used as a substitute for pompano, snapper, or cod. Because its lean meat is a bit dry, it benefits from a tangy sauce or marinade.

Dolphin in Dilly Cheese Sauce

1½ pounds dolphin fillets
3 medium dill pickles, thinly sliced
1 Tbsp. butter or margarine, melted, divided
½ tsp. salt
⅛ tsp. nutmeg
2 Tbsp. butter or margarine
2 Tbsp. flour
1 cup milk
3 oz. process cheese, cubed
¼ tsp. salt
½ tsp. dry mustard
½ tsp. Worcestershire sauce
⅛ tsp. garlic salt

Thaw fillets in the refrigerator if they are frozen. Wipe with damp cloth or paper towel; arrange half of fillets in oiled, shallow baking dish. Cover fillets with a layer of sliced dill pickle; top with remaining fillets. Brush with melted butter or margarine; sprinkle with salt and nutmeg. Bake in preheated 350°F oven 30 minutes or until fish flakes easily with a fork.

Meanwhile, melt butter or margarine in saucepan. Remove from heat and stir in flour. Gradually add milk and cook, stirring constantly, until sauce thickens. Add remaining ingredients; continue cooking until cheese melts. Place fillets on heated platter and pour hot cheese sauce over fish. Serve at once. **Serves 4.**

Old Fashioned Baked Stuffed Dolphin

2 pounds dolphin fillets, fresh or frozen
1½ cups celery, chopped
⅓ cup onion, chopped
¼ cup butter or margarine, melted
½ tsp. salt
½ tsp. poultry seasoning
1¼ quarts soft bread cubes
2 Tbsp. milk
1 egg, beaten
2 Tbsp. butter, melted
½ tsp. paprika
½ tsp. salt

Thaw fish if it is frozen, and wipe it with a damp cloth or paper towel; cut into serving-size portions. Sauté celery and onion in butter until tender. Sprinkle salt and poultry seasoning onto bread cubes; toss well. Add bread cubes to celery-onion mixture; combine milk and egg and pour over bread cubes. Toss lightly to mix well. Spread stuffing in a shallow, well-greased baking pan. Arrange fish in a single layer over stuffing. Mix together butter, paprika, and salt. Cover fish with sauce. Bake in preheated 350°F oven for about 30 minutes, or until fish flakes easily with a fork. Great with cucumber salad dressed with a zingy vinaigrette sauce! **Serves 4 to 6.**

Palm Beach Dolphin-Cheese Souffle

- 1 pound dolphin (or ocean perch) fillets
- 1 quart boiling water
- 1 Tbsp. salt
- 3 Tbsp. butter or margarine
- 3 Tbsp. flour
- ½ tsp. salt
- dash freshly ground pepper
- ¼ tsp. white wine Worcestershire sauce
- 3 drops red hot sauce
- ¾ cup milk
- 4 egg yolks, beaten
- ½ cup process sharp American cheese, grated
- 4 egg whites, beaten

Thaw fillets if frozen. Skin fillets and place in boiling salted water in a large saucepan. Cover and return to a boil; immediately reduce heat and simmer 10 minutes, until fish flakes easily with a fork. Drain; flake fish. Set aside. Melt butter, blend in flour and seasonings. Add milk gradually and cook until thick and smooth, stirring constantly. Stir a little of the heated sauce into the egg yolks; add to the remaining sauce, still stirring constantly. Blend in cheese and fish. Fold in egg whites gently. Pour into well-oiled casserole with high sides. Place casserole in a pan of hot water and bake in preheated 350°F oven for 40 to 45 minutes, until souffle is puffed up and set firmly in center. Serve at once... souffles won't wait! **Serves 6.**

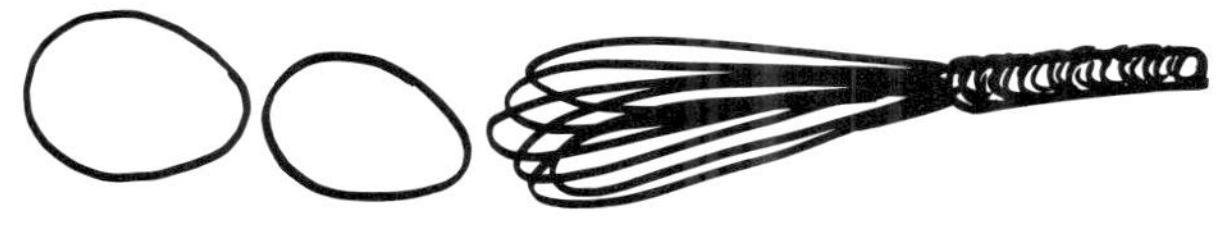

Oven-Fried Dolphin

- 2 pounds dolphin fillets
- ½ cup vegetable oil
- 2 Tbsp. lemon juice
- 1 clove garlic, peeled and quartered
- 1 cup herb-flavored croutons, crushed
- ½ cup Parmesan cheese
- ¼ cup parsley, chopped
- 1 clove garlic, finely chopped

Thaw fish if frozen. Cut fillets into serving size portions and place them in a glass baking dish, about 14 x 9 x 2 inches in size. Combine vegetable oil, lemon juice, and garlic. Pour sauce over fish; refrigerate, covered, for 30 minutes, turning once. Combine crushed croutons, cheese, parsley, garlic. Remove fish from sauce it was marinated in and roll in crumb mixture. Place on a well-greased bake-and-serve platter, about 15 x 10 x 1 inches. Drizzle 2 tablespoons marinade over fish. Bake in oven, preheated to 500°F, for 10 to 15 minutes, or until fish flakes easily. **Serves 4 to 6.**

Dolphin Fillets with Shrimp-Clam Sauce

4 dolphin fillets (or other white fish)
2 cups white wine
4 slices lemon
4 slices onion
1 bay leaf
8 shrimp, shelled
8 clams, shucked
4 whole mushrooms
3 cups medium white sauce (see recipe page 136)
½ tsp. salt
dash pepper

Thaw fish if frozen, and wipe with a damp cloth. Fold each fillet in half. Place in a well-greased baking pan. Cover with wine, lemon, onion and bay leaf. Butter a piece of heavy brown paper and cover the baking dish with it, cutting a small hole in the center. Poach by baking in 350°F oven, covered, for 15 minutes or until fish flakes easily. Drain fish, saving the liquid; keep fish warm in a very low oven. Discard the brown paper. In a pie pan or other shallow pan, broil shrimp, clams and mushrooms for 5 minutes, in the reserved liquid in which the fish was poached. Drain. Season white sauce to taste. Line bottom of broiler-proof casserole with ½ cup of the sauce. Over the sauce, place fillets, shrimp, clams and mushrooms. Top with remaining sauce. Slide under the broiler for a few minutes, until browned lightly. Serve hot. **Serves 4.**

Flounder

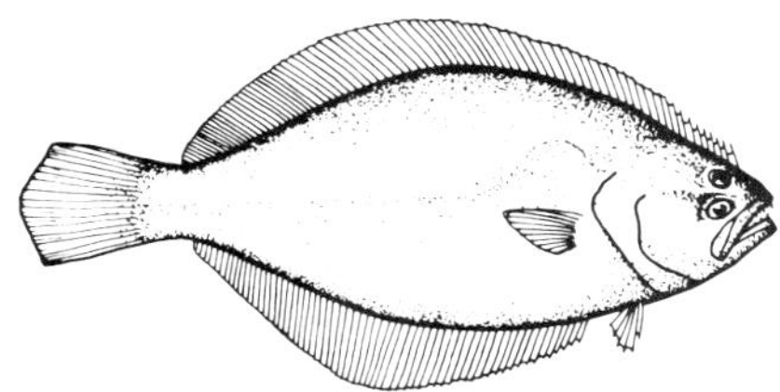

Florida's favorite Southern flounder is caught in shallow coastal waters from North Carolina to Texas, but the largest volume is harvested by shrimp trawlers in the Gulf of Mexico.

Remember the last time you bought fish labelled sole? Fact is, you probably bought flounder. Most white fish sold in fillets is called sole, especially in restaurants. No, you aren't being cheated. It's a bit confusing, but flounder is the generic name for many saltwater fish, such as lemon or gray sole, found in both Atlantic and Pacific waters. Genuine sole from European waters (such as Dover sole) is imported frozen, and must be labelled "imported."

Flounder is a lean fish with a delicate flavor and texture, which is delicious deep-fried, sautéed, baked or steamed. Don't hesitate to substitute it in any recipe calling for sole, or other white fish such as haddock, cod, ocean perch or scrod. It works fine!

Flounder Florentine

6 Tbsp. butter, divided
¼ cup onion, minced
1 clove garlic, minced
2 10-oz. packages frozen spinach, thawed and well drained, OR
1½ cups cooked fresh spinach, chopped and squeezed dry
½ tsp. salt
¼ tsp. pepper
¼ tsp. nutmeg
2 pounds flounder fillets (thawed, if frozen)
½ cup white wine
3 Tbsp. flour
½ tsp. dry mustard
1½ cups skim milk
Parmesan cheese
paprika

Melt 3 tablespoons butter in skillet; add onion and garlic and sauté until transparent but not browned. Stir in spinach, salt, pepper and nutmeg. Rinse fillets in cold water and pat dry. Place 1½ tablespoons spinach on each fillet and roll up. Place fillets, seam side down, in a buttered baking dish, and then pour in the wine. Bake in preheated 350°F oven for 25 to 30 minutes. Remove fish and place in a barely warm oven, reserving ½ cup of cooking liquid.

Melt remaining 3 tablespoons of butter; add flour and mustard. Add milk and the reserved ½ cup cooking liquid. Cook over medium heat, stirring constantly, until sauce boils and thickens. Pour over fish and sprinkle with Parmesan cheese and paprika. If you like, slide this dish under the broiler for a few minutes before serving, until it's bubbly hot... just be sure the dish is broiler-proof! Serve with a crisp green salad splashed with vinaigrette. **Serves 4 to 6.**

Flounder Dumplings with Caper Sauce

1 pound flounder fillets
¼ cup onion, chopped
1½ Tbsp. butter or margarine
2½ cups soft bread crumbs
2 Tbsp. celery, minced
1 Tbsp. parsley flakes
1 tsp. salt
¼ tsp. white pepper
3 Tbsp. grated Parmesan OR sharp Cheddar cheese
1 egg, beaten
¼ cup milk
Caper Sauce (recipe below)

Wipe fish with damp cloth. Put through food chopper or food processor using medium blade. Sauté onion in butter; add to fish. Add bread crumbs, celery, parsley flakes, salt, white pepper, and cheese. Toss lightly. Add egg and milk and mix well.

Shape into 1½-inch balls. Add 1 teaspoon salt to 2 quarts of water and bring to a boil. Add dumplings. Cover tightly and cook until dumplings rise to the surface, about 10 minutes. Remove from water with slotted spoon. Drain and serve hot with Caper Sauce. **Serves 2 to 4.**

Caper Sauce

1 Tbsp. flour
¼ tsp. white pepper
1 Tbsp. capers
2 Tbsp. canned tomato sauce
1 cup chicken or beef stock OR bouillon

Mix together flour, white pepper, capers and tomato sauce. Stir in stock. Heat slowly, stirring occasionally, until slightly thickened. Serve at once with hot dumplings. **Makes 1 cup.**

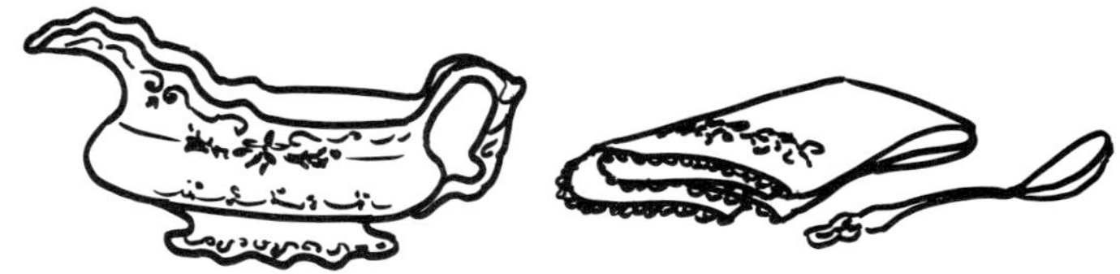

Fillet of Flounder (Sole) Duglere

4 flounder fillets, ½ pound each
1 small onion, sliced
2 Tbsp. parsley, chopped
2-3 Tbsp. celery leaves
½ lemon or lime
1 tsp. salt
1 tsp. butter
pinch pepper
1 quart cold water
2 Tbsp. butter
2 Tbsp. flour
1 medium onion, chopped fine
2 Tbsp. butter
4 large white mushrooms, diced
1 tomato, peeled and chopped
½ cup dry white wine
½ cup Hollandaise sauce
½ cup heavy cream

In a large kettle place fish, sliced onion, parsley, celery leaves, lemon half (with peel), salt, 1 teaspoon butter and pepper. Add water. Bring to a boil, then lower heat and simmer for 10 minutes or until fish flakes with a fork.

In another kettle, melt 2 tablespoons butter; stir in flour. Stir in 1¾ cups strained fish broth. Cook and stir until smooth and thickened. Keep hot, stirring occasionally.

In a third kettle, sauté chopped onion in 2 tablespoons butter until tender but not browned. Add mushrooms and tomato. Sauté 3 or 4 minutes longer. Add white wine. Cook rapidly until almost dry.

Turn vegetable mixture into fish broth sauce. Carefully stir in Hollandaise and heavy cream. Check seasoning and add more salt and pepper, if desired. Place fish fillets in shallow baking pan; pour sauce over fish. Slide under broiler to brown lightly. Serve at once — and listen to the compliments! **Serves 4.**

Flounder Fillets Tropicale

2 Tbsp. cornstarch
½ cup water
¾ cup pineapple syrup, divided (drained from can of pineapple chunks)
1¼ tsp. salt
¼ cup sugar
⅓ cup vinegar
1 Tbsp. soy sauce
paprika
2 lb. flounder fillets, cut into 6 pieces (thawed, if frozen)
2 Tbsp. lemon or lime juice
1¼ cups canned pineapple chunks
¼ cup butter
2 Tbsp. crystallized ginger, minced
1 cup green pepper, cut into strips
1 Tbsp. pimiento, chopped
2 cups water
2 cups rice (packaged, precooked type)

Mix cornstarch and water, blending thoroughly. Combine with ½ cup pineapple syrup, ½ teaspoon salt, sugar, vinegar, soy sauce; set aside. Place fillets in oiled saucepan; sprinkle with paprika. Add remaining pineapple syrup and lemon juice. Cover saucepan, and bring mixture to a boil. Reduce heat and simmer 5 to 10 minutes, until fish flakes with a fork.

Meanwhile, melt butter in large skillet. Add pineapple chunks, ginger, and green pepper. Cook over medium heat for 5 minutes. Drain liquid from fish and add it to the mixture in the skillet. Keep fish warm. Add cornstarch mixture to skillet; bring to a boil, and boil 1 minute, stirring constantly, until sauce is slightly thick and clear. Add pimiento.

Bring water and remaining salt to a boil in another pan. Stir in rice; cover, remove from heat, and let stand 5 minutes. Arrange fish in center of a platter or shallow casserole. Place cooked rice around the edge of the dish and pour pineapple chunk mixture over the fish. **Serves 4 to 6.**

Italian Stuffed Croaker

(Croaker is a less expensive substitute for flounder, trout or perch)

- **3 pounds pan-dressed croaker or one of the fish above, fresh or frozen**
- **¾ cup Italian salad dressing**
- **1 16-oz. can whole tomatoes**
- **¾ cup uncooked rice**
- **¾ teaspoon salt**
- **½ cup onion, chopped**
- **½ cup green pepper, chopped**
- **½ cup celery, chopped**
- **1 4-oz. can mushroom stems and pieces, drained and coarsely chopped**
- **1 clove garlic, minced**
- **3 Tbsp. margarine or cooking oil**
- **½ tsp. salt**
- **½ tsp. leaf oregano**
- **¼ tsp. pepper**
- **1 tsp. salt**

Thaw fish if frozen. Remove fins. Marinate fish in Italian salad dressing in refrigerator for 2 hours, turning once. Break tomatoes into small pieces, removing tough centers, reserving liquid. In 2-quart saucepan, place tomatoes and tomato liquid; bring to a boil. Add rice and ¾ teaspoon salt. Return to boiling point; cover. Reduce heat and cook over low heat 20 to 25 minutes according to package directions. In 10-inch frying pan, cook onion, green pepper, celery, mushrooms and garlic in margarine until tender but not brown. Add rice mixture, ½ teaspoon salt, oregano and pepper. Remove fish from marinade, reserving marinade. Sprinkle inside and outside of fish with 1 teaspoon salt. Stuff fish cavity loosely with rice mixture. Place fish in well-greased baking dish, 13 x 9 x 2 inches. Bake in 350°F oven 25 to 30 minutes or until fish flakes with a fork, basting occasionally during cooking with reserved marinade.

(Note: You may use 2 pounds of fillets instead of pan-dressed fish. Just place fillet in pan, top with stuffing, and cover with another fillet of the same size.) **Serves 6.**

Easy Spaghetti with Fish

2 Tbsp. butter or margarine
¾ cup chopped onion
1 16-oz. pkg. frozen sole fillets, thawed, OR 1 pound fresh sole fillets
salt, pepper
½ cup shredded Cheddar cheese
1 large tomato, cut in wedges
8 oz. spaghetti
3 quarts boiling water
2 Tbsp. chopped parsley

In small saucepan, melt 1 tablespoon butter. Add onion; sauté over medium heat, stirring occasionally, until onion is tender – about 5 minutes.

Lightly sprinkle one side of each fillet with salt and pepper. Cut fillets in half lengthwise. Spread 2 teaspoons sautéed onion and about 1 tablespoon cheese on each fillet half. Reserve remaining onion cheese. Roll up fillets; fasten each with toothpick. Place in lightly buttered 9-inch pie plate; dot fillets with remaining butter. Bake uncovered in 425°F oven 15 minutes. Remove from oven. Sprinkle remaining cheese on top of fillets. Add tomato wedges and bake 5 minutes more, or until fish flakes with a fork.

Meanwhile, gradually add spaghetti and 1 tablespoon salt to rapidly boiling water, so water continues to boil. Cook uncovered, stirring occasionally, until tender. Drain in colander. Toss together cooked spaghetti and remaining reserved onion and parsley. Serve spaghetti on heated platter topped with fish and tomato wedges. **Serves 4.**

Zesty French Fillets

¾ cup celery, chopped
1½ pounds flounder fillets
½ tsp. salt
⅛ tsp. pepper
⅓ cup commercial sour cream
⅓ cup French dressing
1 Tbsp. parsley, minced
2 Tbsp. bread crumbs

Preheat oven to 375°F. Cover the bottom of a 12 x 8 x 2-inch oiled baking dish with chopped celery. Arrange fillets on top; sprinkle with salt and pepper. Cover and bake at 375°F for 25 minutes. Combine sour cream and French dressing. Uncover fillets and spoon off liquid; spread lightly with sour cream mixture; sprinkle with parsley. Scatter bread crumbs on top. Place under preheated broiler until lightly browned. **Serves 6.**

Grouper

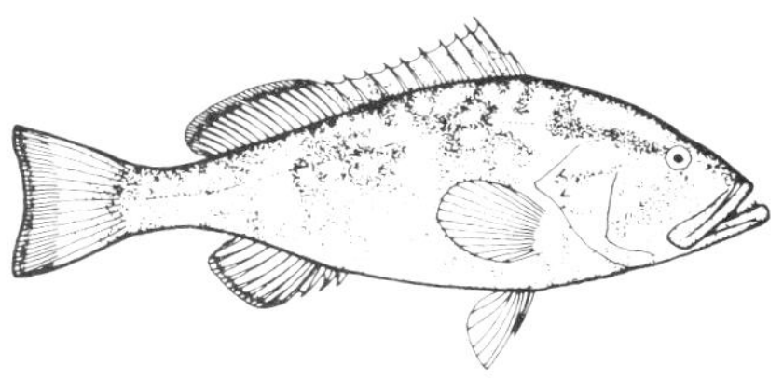

Some 400 different species of the grouper—a member of the sea bass family—thrive in temperate and tropical waters around the world. Three of the most popular in Florida are the Nassau grouper, and the red and black groupers found along Florida coasts, especially around coral reefs.

Grouper is lean and relished for its moist flakiness and sweet taste, especially when deep fried. But old-timers in the Bahamas and in the Florida Keys insist that grouper makes the world's best chowder. An important fact: never eat the roe of the grouper because it is sometimes implicated in ciguatera poisoning. The rest of the fish is fine, with no such problems. Grouper should be skinned before you use it. The steaks, whole fish or fillets may be broiled, baked, or used in combination dishes.

Old South Grouper Chowder

1½ pounds grouper fillets
⅓ cup butter or margarine
2 large onions, chopped
2 green peppers, chopped
2 tsp. salt
2 1-pound cans tomatoes with okra
¼ tsp. pepper
1 bay leaf
1 cup cooked rice

Skin fillets and cut in cubes. If frozen, thaw completely on bottom shelf of the refrigerator. Meanwhile, melt butter in saucepan. Add onions and peppers; cook over low heat for 5 to 10 minutes until tender but not browned. Stir in canned tomatoes with okra, salt, pepper and bay leaf. Cook over low heat 15 minutes or more. (Longer cooking does not hurt gumbo so long as the fish and rice have not yet been added.) About 10 minutes before serving time, add fish cubes and rice to gumbo. Cook for about 8 minutes, or until fish flakes easily with a fork. (For a Creole touch, add a splash of red hot sauce, according to your taste.) **Serves 4.**

Oven-Fried Grouper with Barbecue Sauce

- 2 pounds grouper fillets
- 1 Tbsp. salt
- 1 cup milk
- 1 cup bread crumbs
- 4 Tbsp. butter or margarine, melted
- 1 cup bottled or homemade barbecue sauce

If fish is frozen, thaw in refrigerator. Skin fillets and cut into serving size portions. Add salt to milk; dip fish in milk and roll in crumbs. Place in well-greased baking pan and pour melted butter over fish. Place pan on shelf near the top of a very hot (500°F) oven and bake 10 to 12 minutes, until fish flakes easily with a fork. Turn out onto a warm platter and pour hot barbecue sauce over the fish. **Serves 4 to 6.**

Grouper and Noodles Bearnaise

- 2 pounds skinned grouper fillets, fresh or frozen
- 2 cups butter-flavored cracker crumbs
- ½ tsp. lemon pepper seasoning
- 3 egg whites, beaten
- vegetable oil
- hot cooked noodles
- Bearnaise Sauce (recipe below)

Thaw fillets if frozen; dry. Cut fillets into 1 x 4-inch strips. Combine cracker crumbs and seasoning; mix well. Dip each fish strip into beaten egg whites and roll in cracker crumbs to coat. Brown in vegetable oil heated to 360°F until fish flakes easily when tested with a fork. Drain on paper towels; prepare Bearnaise Sauce. Toss hot noodles with half of sauce. Divide noodles equally on 4 plates. Place grouper over noodles. Spoon sauce over grouper and serve hot. **Serves 4.**

Bearnaise Sauce

- ½ cup butter
- 2½ Tbsp. Chablis or other dry white wine
- 2½ Tbsp. red wine vinegar
- 1 Tbsp. green onions, minced
- ½ tsp. tarragon leaves
- ½ tsp. chervil
- ¼ tsp. white pepper
- 3 egg yolks
- 2 Tbsp. water
- ¼ cup parsley, finely chopped
- 1 tsp. lemon or lime juice
- salt, pepper to taste

Melt butter in small pan; keep warm. In top of double boiler, combine wine, vinegar, onions, tarragon, chervil and pepper. Cook over hot water until almost all liquid evaporates. Cool to lukewarm. In small bowl, beat egg yolks with water; blend in wine mixture.

Return sauce to top of double boiler. Place over hot water and cook, beating constantly with whisk until thick. Remove from heat. Add a tablespoon of butter at a time, whisking well until all butter is absorbed. (Sauce will separate if butter is added too fast or it is heated too quickly.) Add parsley; stir in well. Stir in lemon juice, salt and pepper. Use while warm. **Makes 1 cup.**

Fit for a gourmet: grouper and noodles blessed with Bearnaise.

Grouper Almondine

- **2 pounds grouper fillets**
- **1 Tbsp. lemon or lime juice**
- **1 tsp. salt**
- **⅛ tsp. lemon pepper**
- **1½ cups fresh mushrooms, sliced**
- **½ cup hickory smoked salted almonds, chopped**
- **3 Tbsp. butter or margarine, melted**
- **2 Tbsp. chopped parsley**

Skin fillets; thaw if frozen. Place fillets in a single layer in a well-greased 12 x 9 x 2-inch baking dish. Sprinkle with lemon or lime juice, salt and lemon pepper. Bake in 350°F oven 10 to 12 minutes, or until fish flakes with fork. Remove fish to heated platter. Combine remaining ingredients in 2-quart saucepan; cook over low heat about 7 minutes. Spoon hot mixture over fish; serve at once. **Serves 4 to 6.**

Poached Grouper with Diablo Sauce

2 pounds grouper steaks or fillets
2 cups water
¼ cup lemon or lime juice
1 small onion, thinly sliced
1 tsp. salt
3 peppercorns
2 sprigs parsley, chopped
1 bay leaf
parsley
Diablo Sauce (recipe below)

Skin grouper steaks and thaw if frozen. Remove skin and bones if using fillets. Cut fish into serving size portions. Combine water, lemon juice, onion, salt, peppercorns, parsley and bay leaf in a well-greased 10-inch frying pan and bring to a boil. Reduce heat. Place fish in hot liquid, in a single layer. Cover; simmer 8 to 10 minutes or until fish flakes easily with a fork. Carefully remove to a warm platter, and serve with heated Diablo Sauce. Sprinkle with parsley. (If desired, Hollandaise or another favorite sauce may be substituted.) **Serves 4 to 6.**

Diablo Sauce

⅔ cup chili sauce
3 tsp. lemon juice
1 tsp. white wine Worcestershire sauce

Mix all ingredients together in saucepan and heat.

Mullet

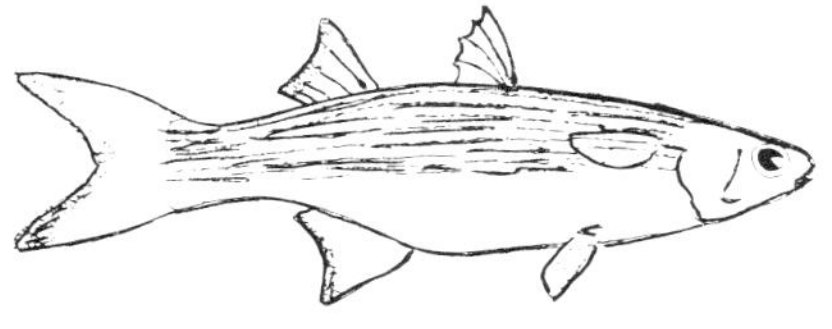

Coastal waters of the Carolinas and Florida yield a plentiful supply of this silvery, acrobatic fish. While some people feel that this rather strong, fatty fish takes a bit of "getting used to," its popularity dates all the way back to the early Romans and Egyptians. It was well-liked by Florida's early settlers and was a staple in the diet of the Spanish and Minorcans, who found many tasty ways to cook it. (Skinning the fish will make it taste milder.)

Mullet is still a great favorite, because it is low in cost and high in protein. It is equally delicious baked, broiled, fried, steamed or barbecued. Slices of smoked mullet on crisp crackers make a tasty appetizer.

Everybody's Favorite Fish Soup

2 pounds mullet fillets, fresh or frozen
1 cup chopped onion
1 cup chopped celery
1 cup chopped green pepper
1 clove garlic, minced
2 Tbsp. cooking oil
1 cup chicken broth
1 28-oz. can tomatoes, undrained
¼ cup white wine
¼ cup chopped parsley
1 tsp. salt
½ tsp. sugar
¼ tsp. basil

Thaw fish if frozen. Skin fillets. Cut into 1-inch cubes. In a 5-quart soup pot, cook onion, celery, green pepper and garlic in oil over medium heat until tender but not browned. Add tomatoes, chicken broth, wine, parsley, salt, sugar and basil; heat to boiling. Reduce heat; cover and simmer 10 minutes. Add fish and cook over low heat 10 minutes or until fish flakes when tested with a fork, stirring occasionally. **Serves 6.**

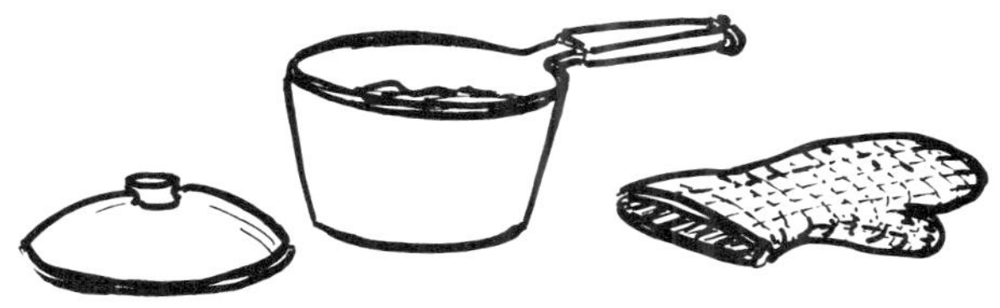

Heavenly Broiled Mullet

2 pounds skinned mullet fillets (or other fish) fresh or frozen
2 Tbsp. lemon juice
¼ cup butter or margarine, softened
½ cup grated Parmesan cheese
3 Tbsp. mayonnaise or salad dressing
3 Tbsp. green onion, chopped
¼ tsp. salt
dash liquid hot pepper sauce

Thaw fish if frozen. Place fillets in single layer on well greased bake-and-serve platter, 15 x 10 inches. Brush fillets with lemon juice. Let stand 10 minutes in refrigerator. Combine remaining ingredients. Broil fillets about 4 inches from source of heat, 6 to 8 minutes or until fish flakes easily with a fork. Remove from heat; spread with cheese mixture. Broil 2 to 3 minutes longer or until lightly browned. **Serves 6.**

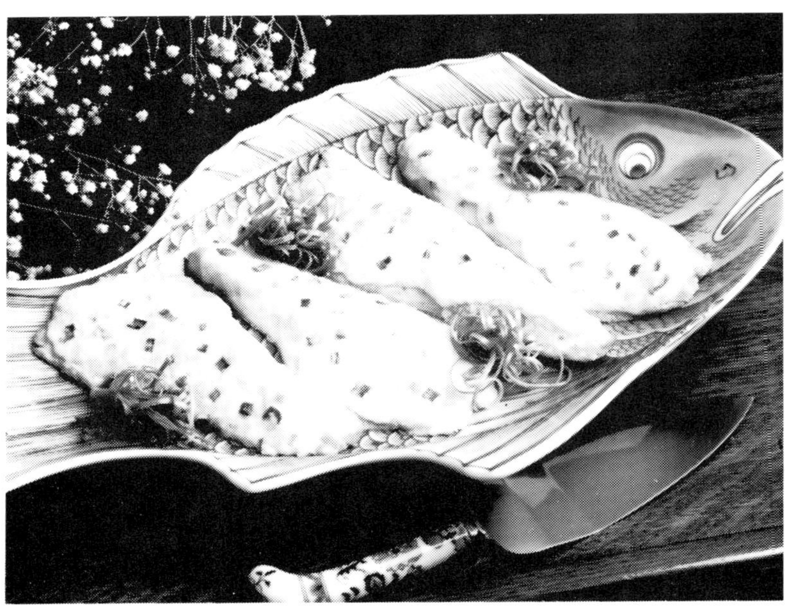

Quick and easy Heavenly Broiled Mullet is dotted with green onion.

Baked Florida Mullet with Hot 'n Sassy Tartar Sauce

3 pounds pan-dressed Florida mullet, OR other pan-dressed fish, fresh or frozen
¾ tsp. liquid hot pepper sauce
1½ tsp. salt
¾ cup Hot 'n Sassy Tartar Sauce
1½ cups unseasoned dry bread crumbs
¼ cup margarine or butter, melted

Thaw fish if frozen. Divide fish into serving size portions. Brush all fish surfaces with liquid hot pepper sauce and sprinkle with salt. Coat all surfaces of fish with tartar sauce. Roll fish in bread crumbs. Place fish on a well-greased baking platter 15 x 9½ x ½ inches. Brush melted margarine over fish. Bake in very hot (450°F) oven 12 to 15 minutes or until fish flakes when tested with a fork. Serve with additional tartar sauce if desired — you may substitute a commercial brand, if you wish. **Serves 6.**

(Note: Mullet vary in size according to season of the year. If pan-dressed mullet are 8 to 10 ounces each, allow one fish per serving. Cut larger mullet into serving size portions. For larger fish, cooking time may be increased — give them the flake test with a fork to be sure they're done.)

Hot 'n Sassy Tartar Sauce

1 cup mayonnaise or salad dressing
2 Tbsp. parsley, chopped
2 Tbsp. sweet pickle, finely chopped, OR drained pickle relish
2 Tbsp. pimiento-stuffed green olives, finely chopped
2 Tbsp. onion, finely chopped
1 tsp. cream-style prepared horseradish
1 tsp. lemon or lime juice
⅛ tsp. white wine Worcestershire
⅛ tsp. salt
dash liquid hot pepper sauce (or more, to be as peppery as you like)

Combine all ingredients; mix well. **Makes 1½ cups sauce.**

Deviled Mullet Fillets

2 pounds mullet fillets
2 Tbsp. vegetable oil
1 Tbsp. Worcestershire sauce
2 Tbsp. prepared mustard
½ cup chili sauce
½ tsp. salt

Rinse and dry fish. Preheat broiler and place fillets in greased broiler pan. Mix other ingredients. Spread evenly over fillets. Broil about 3 inches below heat for about 6 minutes, or until fish flakes easily with a fork. Serve on heated platter, garnished with parsley. **Serves 6.**

Mullet Fillets Paprika

2 pounds mullet fillets (or other fish)
1 tsp. salt
dash pepper
1 tsp. paprika
2 Tbsp. lemon or lime juice
1 tsp. grated onion
2-4 Tbsp. butter or margarine, melted
tomato slices
sweet onion slices

Preheat oven to 350°F. Rinse and cut fillets into serving size pieces. In well-greased baking pan, place fish in single layer, skin side down. Combine salt, pepper, paprika, lemon or lime juice, onion, and melted butter. Pour over mullet. Bake 20 to 25 minutes, or until fish flakes easily when tested with a fork. Serve hot, garnished with slices of tomato and sweet onion. **Serves 6.**

Old-Timey Fish and Grits

1 fresh, fat mullet
1 small, hot green pepper
1 tsp. salt
2 Tbsp. lemon or lime juice
2 Tbsp. parsley, chopped
hot buttered grits

Scale and clean fresh mullet, leaving head and tail intact. In a saucepan, heat ½-inch water and hot pepper until boiling. Slip mullet into pan and immediately lower heat to a simmer. For about 20 minutes (or until fish flakes when tested with a fork), continue to simmer, basting frequently. Add salt to water (to taste), remove from heat and let stand, covered, 5 minutes. Carefully turn fish out onto a heated platter, sprinkle with lemon or lime juice and parsley. Serve with hot buttered grits cooked according to package instructions. **Serves 2.**

Fish and Chips

1½ pounds mullet fillets (thawed, if frozen)
salt and pepper
1 egg, slightly beaten
½ cup milk
1 Tbsp. butter or margarine, melted
¾ tsp. salt
dash cayenne pepper
¾ cup sifted flour
1½ lb. potatoes, peeled and sliced
oil for frying

Rinse fish in cold water and dry with paper towel. Cut in serving-size pieces; sprinkle with salt and pepper. Combine egg, milk, margarine, ¾ teaspoon salt, and dash of cayenne. Add to flour and beat until smooth. Peel potatoes and cut into 6 to 8 pieces. Rinse; dry. Fry in deep, hot oil until well browned. Place potatoes in large pan lined with paper towels; sprinkle with salt, and keep warm in oven. Dip fish into prepared batter and fry in same skillet until crispy brown — 2 or 3 minutes on each side is usually enough. Serve immediately. **Serves 4.**

Oven Barbecued Mullet

⅓ cup vegetable oil or bacon fat, divided
2 pounds mullet fillets (thawed, if frozen)
¾ cup catsup
1 Tbsp. prepared mustard
¼ cup vinegar
1 Tbsp. Worcestershire sauce
2 Tbsp. brown sugar
1 tsp. hickory smoke, OR
 1 tsp. salt
dash hot pepper sauce
paprika
1 large onion, cut into thin slices

Grease shallow pan with part of fat and place fish in pan. Mix remaining fat with catsup, mustard, vinegar, Worcestershire sauce, brown sugar, salt, smoke and hot pepper sauce. Sprinkle fish with paprika. Cover with sliced onion; spread catsup mixture over all.

Preheat oven to 450°F. Place pan on lower rack and bake 10 minutes, basting and adding water if fish becomes dry. Remove pan, turn on broiler unit, and slide pan under broiler for a few minutes to brown lightly just before serving. **Serves 4 to 6.**

Pompano

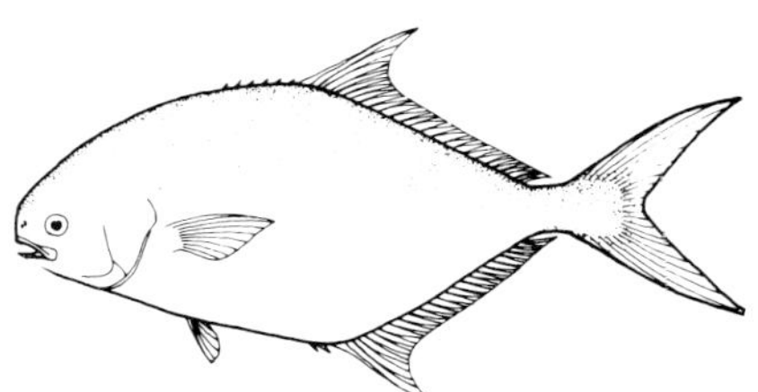

This aristocrat of the sea is thin, with a deeply forked tail and a beautiful silvery skin. It is highly prized for its firm and delicate white flesh, and its price puts it solidly in the luxury range.

Early Spanish fishermen gave the fish its name, which refers to its silvery green color. It thrives in warm waters from North Carolina to Florida and the Gulf of Mexico. It may be steamed, baked, grilled or broiled, but simple treatment is best for this slightly fatty fish — especially broiling while basting with a flavored butter. Greek fishermen in Tarpon Springs use fine grade olive oil to add robust flavor to the delicate fish. But the most popular dish is probably Louisiana's Pompano en Papillote — pompano baked in paper envelopes, enlivened with a Creole seafood sauce.

If you are not lucky enough to have pompano, you may substitute red snapper or cod in a recipe, but of course you won't duplicate the inimitable pompano flavor.

Pompano Almondine

2½ pounds pompano fillets
2 Tbsp. butter or margarine
2 Tbsp. blanched almonds, slivered
1 Tbsp. paprika
2 Tbsp. butter or margarine
Sauce Meuniere (recipe below)

Place fillets in greased, broiler-proof, flat pan. Dot with butter and sprinkle with paprika. Broil 2 inches below heat until fish is easily flaked with fork but still moist. Sauté almonds in butter until golden brown, stirring frequently. Pour hot Sauce Meuniere over fish and sprinkle with almonds. **Serves 4 to 6.**

Sauce Meuniere

½ stick butter
juice of ½ lemon or lime
1 tsp. chopped parsley
dash white wine Worcestershire sauce

Melt butter in a small pan; add lemon juice, parsley, Worcestershire. Stir to blend.

Pompano en Papillote

6 pompano fillets
2 Tbsp. olive oil
1 small onion, finely chopped
¼ tsp. dried thyme
1 tsp. salt
dash freshly ground pepper
½ cup dry white wine
1 lemon, sliced
1 onion, finely chopped
2 Tbsp. butter
2 Tbsp. all-purpose flour
2 egg yolks
1 cup mushrooms, fresh or canned, chopped
½ cup cooked shrimp, finely chopped
¼ tsp. anchovy paste
¼ tsp. powdered mace
juice of 1 lemon or lime
¼ cup truffles, finely chopped (optional)

Pour olive oil in shallow baking dish and lay fish on top. Sprinkle with onion, thyme, salt and pepper. Brown lightly in preheated 350°F oven, turning once; take great care to keep fillets whole. Add white wine and lemon slices. Cover tightly and return to oven, reducing heat to 300°F, to poach for 10 minutes.

Cut 6 squares parchment paper or aluminum foil 12 x 14 inches each. Cut each piece in a large heart shape: fold paper in half and cut, then open out flat. Lightly butter inside; reserve. Remove fillets from pan; set aside. Strain fish stock from pan into large glass measuring cup. Add water to equal 1½ cups. Set stock aside.

Sauté onion in butter in large, heavy saucepan over low heat until transparent. Gradually add flour, stirring until well blended. Cook for 1 minute, stirring constantly. Gradually add strained fish stock; cook over medium heat, stirring constantly, until slightly thickened. To mixture, gradually add egg yolks, continuing to stir. Stir in mushrooms, shrimp, anchovy paste, mace, lemon juice and truffles, if used. Stir over low heat until thickened.

Place a fillet on each square of parchment or foil, being careful not to break it up. Pour sauce over fillet and seal, folding so that folded edges are on the bottom. Place on oiled baking sheet in preheated 400°F oven 10 minutes or until bags are puffed and lightly browned. Place bags on dinner plates and cut open to serve — but be careful of the steam! **Serves 6.**

Florida Pompano in Wine Sauce

1 Florida orange
4 pompano fillets
½ tsp. salt
dash freshly ground pepper
1 Tbsp. butter
1 Tbsp. onion, chopped
½ cup dry white wine
1 cup white sauce (see pg. 136)
¼ cup sherry
½ tsp. ground ginger
1 lime, sliced
paprika

While orange is whole, cut off slivers of rind until you have 2 tablespoons; set aside. Peel orange and divide into segments to use for garnish. Season fish with salt and pepper. In large, shallow saucepan, combine butter, onion, white wine and orange slivers. Bring to a boil, add fish, and boil gently 8 to 10 minutes, until fish flakes easily with a fork. Place fish on heated serving dish and keep warm in very low oven. Strain pan liquid and add to white sauce, stirring until well blended. Add sherry and ginger and cook a scant minute or two, until heated through. Pour sauce over and around pompano fillets and sprinkle with paprika. Garnish with orange sections and lime slices. **Serves 4.**

Old Key West Pompano Stew

½ pound white bacon
2 medium onions, chopped
1 clove garlic, minced
1 small green pepper, chopped
3 stalks celery, chopped
4 medium potatoes, peeled, diced
1½ quarts water
3 pounds pompano steaks
1 tsp. salt
⅛ tsp. pepper (or more, to taste)
2 Tbsp. flour
1 Tbsp. cold water

Dice white bacon; fry until crisp in a large iron pot. Set aside. Fry onions, garlic, green pepper, and celery in bacon drippings over low to medium heat until tender, stirring occasionally. Add potatoes and water. Cover; cook until potatoes are tender, about 25 minutes. Add pompano, salt and pepper. Cover and cook about 15 minutes, or until fish flakes easily with a fork, over low heat. Add flour to a tablespoon of cold water, stir to blend and pour into stew. Stir gently until broth thickens. Serve hot with warm, buttered Cuban bread. **Serves 6.**

Sea Trout

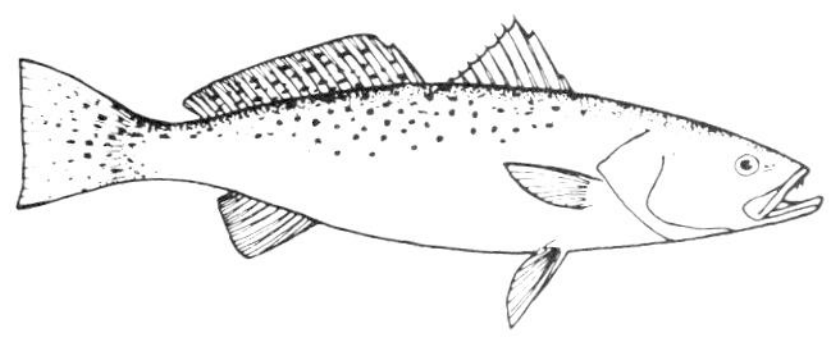

One of my happiest experiences is drifting over the grass beds in Florida Bay, off Rock Harbor in the Florida Keys, where speckled little sea trout respond to a popping cork and a good bite of shrimp from June to December. The sea trout's nickname, weakfish, is derived from the fact that the sea trout has a fragile mouth that easily tears away from a hook.

This slender fish has many black spots, and the white, finely textured, lean meat is exceptionally tasty. What a meal it makes, deep-fried, with a big dollop of hot grits, crunchy hushpuppies and a fresh green salad! It is delicious steamed, baked, grilled, broiled, sautéed, fried or braised... very versatile! It can be substituted in recipes calling for grouper, snapper or whiting.

Now that quick-freezing has been perfected, sea trout can be enjoyed year round. Also, if you buy freshly caught sea trout, be sure to ask for the roe. It is very good and freezes beautifully. Both roe and sea trout (or weakfish) should be iced immediately after being caught, or the delicate flavor and elasticity of the meat will be lessened.

Sea Trout in Dill Butter

1 2-pound sea trout, dressed
1½ tsp. salt
¼ tsp. pepper
½ cup butter or margarine
2 tsp. dillweed
3 Tbsp. lemon juice

Thaw fish if frozen. Clean, rinse well under running water and pat dry. Cut fish almost through, lengthwise, and spread open. Sprinkle with salt and pepper. Melt butter in 10-inch frying pan. Add dill weed. Place fish in single layer, flesh side down, in hot dill butter. At moderate heat, fry for 2 to 3 minutes. Turn carefully, and fry 2 minutes more or until fish flakes easily when tested with a fork. Place fish on warm serving platter. Keep warm in very low oven. When all of fish has been fried, turn heat very low; stir in lemon juice. Pour sauce over fish and serve at once. **Serves 4.**

Peruvian Seviche

(Appetizer)

2 pounds sea trout fillets (or snapper)
½ cup lime juice
1 tsp. salt
⅛ tsp. hot pepper sauce (or more, to taste)
½ cup grapefruit juice
1½ Tbsp. onion, minced
1½ Tbsp. green pepper, minced
1 tsp. chives, snipped
1 Spanish onion, sliced thinly
2 scallions, chopped
½ red pimiento, chopped fine
½ green pepper, chopped fine
2 Tbsp. kernel corn, cooked
grapefruit sections

Cut sea trout into bite-sized pieces. Marinate 12 hours in lime juice with salt and hot pepper sauce. Add grapefruit juice and place minced onion, pepper and chives in marinating liquid. Arrange fish in deep dish with marinade and place Spanish onion in center, on top of fish. Mix scallions, pimiento and green pepper (which have been chopped very fine) and sprinkle them over the fish. Top with a scattering of the corn. Garnish with grapefruit. Chill thoroughly. To serve, guests spear bites of the well-chilled appetizer bites and enjoy them with crisp crackers. (Note: No, the fillets are not cooked. The action of the lime juice "cooks" the meat without the need of heat. If you like, add the fiery taste of jalapeño peppers to the marinade. Peruvians enjoy shedding a few tears as they feast on Seviche!) **Serves 6 to 8.**

Fried Trout in Cream

4 slices bacon
4 1-pound sea trout, cleaned
1 cup all-purpose flour
1 tsp. salt
½ tsp. pepper
1 cup light cream

In heavy iron frying pan, fry bacon until crisp and brown. Remove, drain on paper towels, and crumble; set aside. Dredge trout in mixture of flour, salt and pepper; place in frying pan in bacon drippings. Fry 2 to 3 minutes on each side, until lightly browned. Add cream. Cook over low heat (simmer) for 2 minutes, just until hot and bubbly. Slide fish, in pan, under preheated broiler until lightly browned. Turn out onto heated serving platter. Sprinkle with crumbled bacon and serve at once. **Serves 4.**

Easy Spaghetti with Fish, page 34.

Above: Italian Stuffed Croaker, page 33.
Top right: Lettuce-Baked Lobster Tails, page 85.
Bottom right: Shrimp Ratatouille, page 110.

Above: Broiled Rock Shrimp, page 108.
Top left: Everybody's Favorite Fish Soup, page 39.
Bottom left: Scallops Oriental, page 99.

Above: Oysters Casino, page 95.
Top right: Oriental Shrimp Salad, page 109.
Bottom right: Basil Broiled Snapper, page 59.

Above: Party Time Shrimp Dip, page 104.

Left: Crabber's Creation, page 80.

Baked Trout Parmesan

4 1-pound sea trout, cleaned
½ cup milk
½ cup cornmeal
4 Tbsp. butter or margarine
Parmesan Sauce (recipe below)

Thaw fish if frozen. Wash and pat dry with paper towel. Pour milk into bowl; put cornmeal in pie pan. Dip trout in milk, then roll in cornmeal until well covered. Sauté in butter 2 to 3 minutes on each side, until well browned, adding more butter if necessary. Carefully place fish on broiler-proof serving dish and keep warm in very low oven. Prepare sauce; pour over trout. Slide trout under preheated broiler until lightly browned and bubbly. **Serves 4.**

Parmesan Sauce

2 Tbsp. butter or margarine
2 Tbsp. flour
½ tsp. salt
dash freshly ground pepper
1 cup milk
1 Tbsp. capers
½ cup Parmesan cheese, grated

Melt butter in saucepan; stir in flour, salt and pepper. Gradually stir in milk, followed by capers and cheese. Cook, stirring constantly, until thickened.

A Cocoa fisherman with a fine catch of sea trout, found all along Florida coasts and in the Florida Keys.

Red Snapper

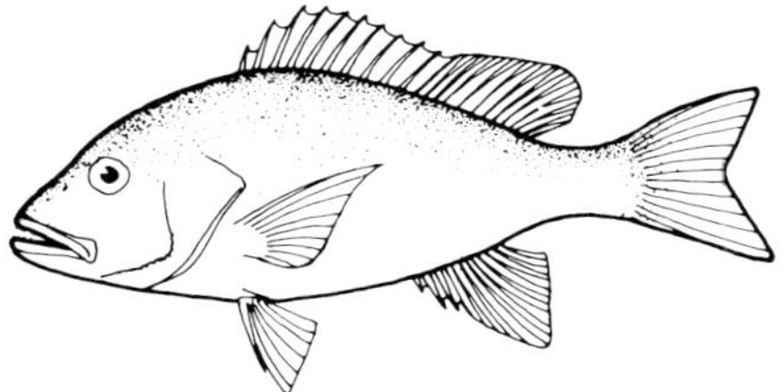

Snapper has snowy white meat–sweet, moist and firm–with mild but distinctive flavor. It's a lean fish, delicious broiled, baked, sautéed, deep-fried, steamed, or poached.

Pensacola (on Florida's northwest coast) is headquarters for much of the snapper caught in the warm Gulf, in deep water. Weighing as little as five pounds to as much as 40 pounds, this beautiful, rosy-colored fish is extremely popular with gourmets, and is one of some 15 species of snapper found in Gulf and Atlantic waters.

Delicate-tasting Gulf red snapper should not be confused with the oily, less meaty snapper from the west coast of the U.S. From more shallow waters come the gray, yellowtail and mutton snappers, none of which equal the fine taste of the red snapper.

Pensacola's fish lovers do intriguing things with this fish. The red head is put in a pot, as a base for fish stock. The meat-filled jowls are served as a local delicacy–fried snapper throats. They also cook them stuffed with cashew nuts or chopped into broth for a slow-cooking gumbo. For frying, broiling, or sautéing, please see the chapter on How to Cook Fish.

Santa Rosa Island Snapper Fillets

(Garlicky and good!)

3 pounds red snapper fillets
½ tsp. salt (or more, to taste)
⅛ tsp. pepper
juice of 1 lemon
1 tsp. oregano
3 cloves garlic
3 Tbsp. olive oil

Sprinkle fillets with salt, pepper, lemon juice and oregano. Place in oiled baking pan and bake in 350°F oven for 30 to 40 minutes, or until fish flakes easily when touched with a fork. Meanwhile, in skillet, sauté minced garlic in hot olive oil until transparent but not browned. Pour hot oil and garlic over the fish and serve hot. Great with a baked potato and sour cream! **Serves 6.**

Pensacola Red Snapper Stuffed with Cashews

1 3½- to 4-pound snapper, whole, cleaned
⅓ cup lime juice
⅓ cup dry white wine
½ tsp. salt
6 Tbsp. butter
½ cup celery, diced
1 green onion, minced
½ clove garlic, minced
2 cups day-old bread crumbs
1½ cups cashew nuts, chopped
dash nutmeg
¼ cup parsley, minced
½ tsp. lemon rind, grated
⅛ tsp. thyme
1 cup dry white wine
minced parsley (for garnish)

Sprinkle fish with lime juice; brush with wine and sprinkle with salt. Place in china bowl, covered, and refrigerate about 2 hours. In skillet, sauté celery, onion and garlic in butter until transparent but not browned, about 5 minutes. Mix together bread crumbs, nuts, nutmeg, parsley, lemon rind and thyme; add to sautéed vegetables. Stuff fish lightly and tie with cord. Place in oiled baking pan; bake in 350°F oven 45 minutes, basting often with 1 cup wine. Serve hot, sprinkled with parsley. **Serves 6 to 8.**

Basil Broiled Snapper

2 pounds skinless snapper fillets, OR other skinless fillets, fresh or frozen
¼ tsp. salt
⅛ tsp. pepper
4 Tbsp. melted margarine
1 Tbsp. soy sauce
1 Tbsp. lemon juice
Basil Butter

Thaw fish if frozen. Sprinkle fish with salt and pepper. Place fish in a single layer on well-greased broiler pan, 12 x 8 x 2 inches. Combine margarine, soy sauce and lemon juice. Brush half of sauce on top side of fish. Broil about 4 inches from heat 4 to 5 minutes. Turn carefully; brush with remaining sauce. Broil 4 to 5 minutes longer or until fish flakes easily when tested with a fork. Top hot fish with Basil butter. **Serves 6.**

Basil Butter

½ cup margarine or butter, softened
1 Tbsp. dried basil

Combine margarine with basil; mix well. Makes ½ cup.

Mild delicate red snapper is rolled in lasagne noodles and served cold on Bibb lettuce — scrumptious!

Red Snapper 'n Pasta Pinwheels

1½ pounds cooked, flaked red snapper, fresh or frozen (or other mild, lean fish)
1 cup mayonnaise
½ cup celery, finely minced
½ cup green onion, finely minced
½ cup deli-style dill pickle, finely minced
¼ cup almonds, toasted and slivered
2 tsp. Dijon mustard
1 tsp. salt
½ tsp. white pepper
¼ tsp. dried dillweed
9 large lasagne noodles
2 tsp. paprika
Bibb lettuce, for garnish

Thaw fish if frozen. In medium mixing bowl, combine all ingredients except noodles, paprika and lettuce. Mix well. Cook noodles as package directs. Drain, pat dry; arrange flat on board. Spread filling over noodles, leaving a one inch border on one short end. From borderless end, roll noodles up tightly; dip curly edges in paprika. Place noodles seam side down on tray. Cover; chill 2 hours. To serve, arrange lettuce on plates; cut each roll in half and arrange with cut side down on lettuce. **Serves 6.**

Steamed Red Snapper with Vegetables

- 2 6-oz. red snapper fillets, fresh or frozen
- ½ tsp. salt
- ⅛ tsp. pepper
- ¼ pound fresh pea pods, trimmed
- 1 carrot, cut into thin strips
- 8 small fresh mushrooms, sliced
- 1 clove garlic, minced
- 4 lemon slices

Thaw fillets if frozen. Wipe with damp cloth. Cut cooking parchment paper into sheets to fold around fillets, about 12 inches square. (Use aluminum foil if you have no parchment.) Place each fillet in middle of parchment; sprinkle with salt and pepper. Divide remaining ingredients; place atop fillets. Fold up parchment so that sides are sealed and ends are tucked under. With ends on bottom, place on baking sheet and bake in preheated 400°F oven about 15 minutes. Cut open carefully (watch for steam!) and serve in parchment paper. **Serves 2.**

Red Snapper in Florida Citrus Sauce

- 2 pounds red snapper fillets, fresh or frozen
- 3 Tbsp. Florida orange juice
- 2 Tbsp. orange liqueur (optional)
- 1 Tbsp. orange rind, grated
- 1 tsp. Florida lime juice
- 5 Tbsp. butter or margarine, melted
- ¼ tsp. salt (or more, to taste)
- ⅛ tsp. pepper
- ¼ tsp. nutmeg
- parsley for garnish

Thaw fillets if frozen. Place fillets in a well-greased baking pan, in a single layer. Combine remaining ingredients; pour over fish. Bake in preheated 350°F oven 25 to 30 minutes, or until fish flakes easily with a fork. Remove to warm serving dish, pour pan sauces over fish, garnish with parsley and serve hot. **Serves 4.**

Snappy Broiled Snapper

2 pounds skinless red snapper fillets, fresh or frozen
½ cup frozen orange juice concentrate, thawed
¼ cup vegetable oil
¼ cup soy sauce
¼ cup cider vinegar
½ tsp. salt
dash freshly ground pepper
chopped parsley, for garnish

Thaw fillets if frozen. Cut fillets into 6 portions. Place fish in a single layer, skinned side up, in well-oiled 15 x 10 x 1-inch baking pan. Combine remaining ingredients, except parsley. Brush fish with sauce. Broil about 4 inches from source of heat 5 minutes. Turn fish carefully and brush with sauce. Broil additional 5 to 7 minutes, or until fish is lightly browned and flakes easily when tested with a fork. Sprinkle with parsley. **Serves 6.**

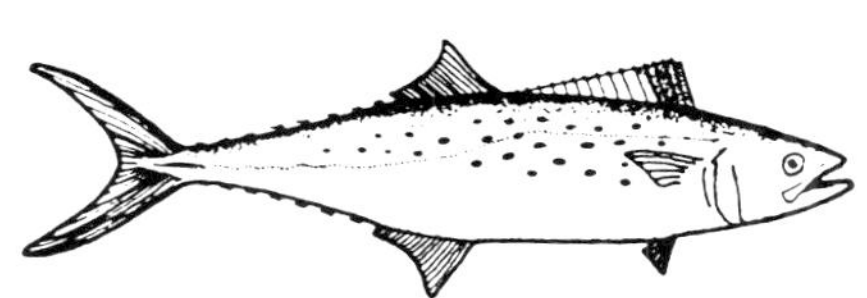

Spanish Mackerel

This glistening blue-black fish has reddish meat that turns an ivory color when cooked. Averaging three to four pounds, it thrives in waters around Florida and in the Gulf of Mexico. Its strong, fishy odor marries well with a tart sauce or marinade such as acidic wine or tomato sauce. Like all fatty fish, mackerel should be eaten as fresh as possible. You may substitute mullet or bluefish for Spanish mackerel.

The good news from medical researchers is that Spanish mackerel (because of its Omega-3 fatty acids that help prevent heart attacks) is one of the most healthful fish we can eat. It is delicious braised, smoked, grilled, sautéed, deep-fried and poached. A helpful tip: to broil mackerel in the oven, place the fillets skin side down and top with a little flavored butter.

Broiled Mackerel, Red and Hot

2 pounds mackerel fillets
1 tsp. salt
dash freshly ground black pepper
1 cup grated sharp cheese
3 Tbsp. chili sauce
1 Tbsp. prepared Dijon mustard
2 tsp. horseradish (or more to taste)
¼ cup butter or margarine, melted

Thaw fish if frozen, wipe with a damp cloth and cut into serving portions. Sprinkle both sides with salt and pepper. Combine cheese, chili sauce, mustard and horseradish. Place fish on greased broiler pan about 2 inches below heating unit. Brush with butter; broil 5 to 8 minutes or until lightly browned. Turn carefully and brush other side with butter; broil 5 to 8 minutes longer, or until fish flakes easily with a fork. Spread cheese mixture on top of fish. Slide under broiler just long enough for cheese to melt and brown lightly — 1 to 2 minutes. (This fish can be as hot-tasting as you like. For a real taste-tingler, just add more horseradish!) **Serves 4 to 6.**

Mackerel Salad Oriental

- 1 Florida lime
- 4 Spanish mackerel fillets
- 5 whole black peppercorns
- ¼ cup sauterne wine
- ½ tsp. powdered dill
- ½ cup French dressing, divided
- 2 hard-cooked eggs
- ½ cup celery, chopped
- 1 cup canned bean sprouts, drained
- 8 canned water chestnuts, drained, sliced
- ¼ cup cucumber, chopped
- ¼ cup green pepper, chopped
- 2-4 dashes hot pepper sauce
- lettuce

Squeeze lime juice over fish and let stand in refrigerator 15 minutes or more. In a saucepan, combine sauterne, peppercorns and dill, along with enough water to cover mackerel. Heat to a simmer; add mackerel. Poach until fish flakes easily, 8 to 12 minutes, depending on thickness of fillets. Drain fish and refrigerate in glass dish, tightly covered. When thoroughly cooled, flake and pour ¼ cup French dressing over fish. Cover and refrigerate at least one hour more.

Separate egg whites from yolks and chop whites. Combine flaked fish, chopped egg whites, bean sprouts, water chestnuts, celery, cucumber and green pepper. Splash on desired amount of hot pepper sauce and enough French dressing to moisten. Toss lightly and serve on lettuce, with sieved hard-cooked egg yolks sprinkled on top. (To reduce cholesterol, eliminate the egg yolks and sprinkle with chopped parsley.) **Serves 4.**

Oven-Fried Mackerel Steaks

- 4 mackerel steaks
- 2 tsp. salt
- ⅛ tsp. pepper
- 1 cup milk
- ¾ cup fine, dry bread crumbs
- 4 Tbsp. butter or margarine, melted

If frozen, thaw steaks in refrigerator. Mix milk with salt and pepper. Place crumbs in separate shallow bowl. Dip fish in milk and then roll in the crumbs. Place the fish in a well-greased baking pan and pour the melted butter over it. Bake in preheated, 500°F oven 10 to 20 minutes, or until flakes easily. (For cooking time, figure about 10 minutes for each inch of the fish's thickest point.) Serve at once on a heated platter. Looks nice garnished with radish roses. **Serves 4.**

Mackerel with Veggie Sauce

2 2-pound whole Spanish mackerel
2 stalks celery, sliced
1 large onion, chopped
1 tomato, peeled, chopped
1 large carrot, chopped
¾ cup cider vinegar
½ green pepper, seeded, chopped
½ tsp. salt
1 Tbsp. parsley, chopped
¼ tsp. thyme
1 bay leaf

Keep mackerel refrigerated until ready to use. In saucepan, combine all ingredients except fish, and add just enough water to cover vegetables. Cook at a simmer for 20 minutes; remove bay leaf. In well-greased baking dish, place mackerel; pour vegetable sauce over fish. In preheated, 400°F oven, bake about 20 minutes, or until fish flakes easily with a fork. In a heated serving dish, pour a little sauce, place fish on this, and then pour the balance of vegetable sauce over. Serve hot. Very good with rice pilaf! **Serves 6.**

Baked Mackerel, Spanish Style

2 pounds Spanish mackerel fillets (or mullet)
1 Tbsp. oil
1 cup onion, thinly sliced
1½ tsp. salt
¼ tsp. freshly ground pepper
¼ tsp. nutmeg
dash cayenne
2 large tomatoes, peeled and sliced
2 Tbsp. snipped chives
1 3-oz. can mushrooms, sliced
1 Tbsp. dry white wine
½ tsp. brown gravy sauce (bottled)
¼ cup buttered bread crumbs

Use oil to grease large, shallow baking dish suitable for serving at table. Arrange onion over bottom of the dish, then place fish in single layer over onion. Sprinkle with salt, pepper, nutmeg and cayenne blended together. Top with sliced tomatoes; sprinkle with chives. Combine mushrooms and their liquid with wine and brown gravy sauce; pour over fish.

Bake in preheated 400°F oven 15 minutes. Over top, sprinkle the buttered bread crumbs. Bake 15 minutes more, until fish flakes easily and bread crumbs are nicely browned. This is a perfect dish to serve with rice, guacamole (mashed avocado flavored with onion and hot pepper sauce) and wonderful, crusty, fresh-baked Cuban bread — plus steaming cups of the inimitable black, strong and potent Cuban coffee. **Serves 4.**

Oven Barbecued Spanish Mackerel

- ½ cup vegetable oil
- 2 Tbsp. lemon or lime juice
- ¼ cup catsup
- 1 tsp. Worcestershire sauce
- 2 Tbsp. onion, minced
- ½ tsp. salt
- 2 pounds Spanish mackerel fillets

Mix together oil, lemon juice, catsup, Worcestershire sauce, onion and salt. Thaw fish fillets if frozen, preferably in the refrigerator. Arrange fillets in a well-greased broiler pan. Spoon sauce over fillets, covering meat well. Place pan 4 to 5 inches from heating unit and broil 5 minutes or until fish flakes easily with a fork. You might like this as a sandwich served over toasted hamburger buns, with a good tart cole slaw. **Serves 6.**

This delicious Key West feast includes Florida's own sea trout, shrimp, stone crab claws, citrus and avocado.

Florida Shellfish Recipes

Clams

New England has the soft clam, while the hard clam (called quahog by the Indians) is plentiful on the shores of North Carolina and Florida. Hard shell clams have three names: littlenecks (1 to 2 inches wide), cherrystones (2 to 3 inches wide) and chowder clams (more than 3 inches wide). All hard shell clams are the same, except for the size.

Littlenecks and cherrystones are delicious raw or cooked and are often served on the half-shell. Because they are tough when raw, the chowder clams are usually cooked and chopped before they are used.

How to Open Clams

It's important to use only tightly closed clams, to ensure their freshness. One easy way to open them is to put them in the freezer for 20 minutes, and then open them with a short, heavy knife. Force the knife between the lips of the shell near the hinge angled slightly upward, and cut the flesh free from the top of the shell. Run the knife under the flesh in the bottom shell to free it. Slowly pry the shells apart and discard the top shell, but be careful — don't spill the delicious juice! Chill and serve clams within one hour of opening. Great with a splash of Florida lime juice and horseradish or black pepper to taste.

Clam "Dunk"

2 3-oz. packages cream cheese
1 cup minced clams
2¼ tsp. clam liquid
½ tsp. salt
dash pepper
½ tsp. prepared horseradish

Blend softened cream cheese with clams, clam liquid, salt, pepper and horseradish. Use as dip or spread, with crisp vegetables or crackers. Keep cold; serve on crushed ice. **Makes 1½ cups.**

Steamed Clams

4 quarts soft-shell clams (steamers)
½ cup boiling water
juice of ½ lemon
½ lb. (2 sticks) butter or margarine
½ lemon, thinly sliced

Scrub clams under running cold water to remove all sand. Drop clams into large steamer kettle holding ½ cup boiling water. Cover and steam just until clams open — 5 to 10 minutes.

Melt butter or margarine; add juice of ½ lemon and place in serving bowl. For each serving, heap clams in soup dish. Pour hot broth from kettle, strained through cheesecloth, into individual cups. Float a lemon slice in each cup of broth. Guests dip each clam into hot broth and then into melted lemon butter. Don't forget the paper bibs! **Serves 4.**

New England Clam Chowder

2 dozen medium quahog clams, OR
2 7½-oz. cans clams, OR
  1 pint shucked clams
1 cup water
1 tsp. pickling spices
½ cup clam liquid
1½ cups water
¼ pound salt pork, minced
1 cup celery, diced
4 cups potatoes, peeled and diced
3 medium onions, diced
1¾ cups milk
1 cup light cream
2 Tbsp. all-purpose flour
dash black pepper

Pour 1 cup water into kettle and add pickling spices. Add clams, cover, and bring to a boil. Reduce heat; simmer just until shells open — 5 to 10 minutes. Drain, saving liquid. Remove clams from shells and dice. Set aside.

Grill or fry minced salt pork until brown; set aside and save fat. To the fat, add ½ cup clam liquid, 1½ cups water, celery, potatoes and onion. Cook, covered, for 15 to 20 minutes, until potatoes are tender. Blend 2 tablespoons water with flour; stir into chowder. Cook, stirring, until mixture boils. Season to taste with salt and pepper. Add clams, milk and cream. Reduce heat and cook just until clams are heated through, and no more. Serve hot with salt pork bits sprinkled on top, plus paprika. **Serves 6.**

Fried Clams

1 quart shucked clams
1 egg, beaten
2 Tbsp. milk
1 tsp. salt
dash pepper
1 cup bread or cracker crumbs
fat or vegetable oil

Drain clams. Combine egg, milk, salt and pepper. Dip clams in egg mixture; roll in crumbs. Fry in heavy skillet containing 1 inch fat or vegetable oil heated to hot but not smoking (365°F on a deep-fat frying thermometer). Cook clams on each side about 5 minutes or until nicely browned. Drain on paper towel. Serve hot. **Serves 6.**

Manhattan Clam Chowder

2 dozen medium quahog clams, OR
  2 7½-oz. cans clams, OR
  1 pint shucked clams
1 cup water
4 ounces salt pork, diced
¼ cup (1 stick) butter or margarine
1 cup celery, finely diced
2 large onions, diced
2 cloves garlic, finely chopped
4 medium, ripe tomatoes, diced, OR
  1 16-oz. can chopped, peeled tomatoes
2 cups diced potatoes
2 Tbsp. all-purpose flour
2 Tbsp. cold water
4 Tbsp. sherry (optional)
⅛ tsp. thyme

For clams with shells, wash thoroughly to remove sand. Place clams in kettle with 1 cup water. Cover; bring to boil. Reduce heat; steam just until shells open, 5 to 10 minutes. Remove clams from shells; dice finely. Strain liquid; save ½ cup. Sauté diced salt pork; set aside. In butter, cook celery, onion and garlic until tender but not browned. Add 3 cups water, ½ cup clam liquid, tomatoes, potatoes, salt and pepper to taste. Cover; simmer 30-35 minutes. Blend flour with 2 tablespoons cold water and stir into chowder. Stir in sherry and thyme. Add clams and cook just until clams are heated through — no longer. Serve hot. **Serves 8.**

Spaghetti with White Clam Sauce

4 **Tbsp. butter or margarine**
2 **cups ground or minced clams, OR**
2 **7½-oz. cans minced clams, undrained**
1 **clove garlic, chopped finely**
1 **tsp. spaghetti sauce seasoning**
½ **cup dry white wine**
½ **16-oz. package spaghetti**
2 **cups boiling salted water**
½ **cup Parmesan cheese, grated**
½ **cup slivered almonds, toasted**

In heavy frying pan, sauté garlic in butter for a couple of minutes; add spaghetti sauce seasoning and wine. Bring to boil; reduce heat and simmer 15 minutes. Meanwhile, boil spaghetti in salted water as directed. Drain, and rinse in cold water. Place 1 tablespoon butter in spaghetti pan to melt. Return spaghetti to pan and heat, stirring around until it dries a bit, 2 to 4 minutes. Add clams to sauce and just heat through. Place spaghetti on platter, top with clam sauce, Parmesan cheese, and almonds. **Serves 6.**

Conch

Since early days, meat from the beautiful conch shell has been a staple in the diet of the Bahamas and the Florida Keys — so much so that Keys folk were nicknamed "Conchs." Because the once-plentiful Queen Conch is threatened, it is illegal to take one from Florida waters. There are, however, other native conch species which are edible.

Today, fresh conch meat is rare. Conch is most often found in the frozen food section at the market. The flavor is delightful, but unless you prepare a long and slow-cooking recipe, the tough meat must be tenderized. Some people pound it with the edge of a plate; or, they drop the conch into boiling water for a couple of minutes, and then pound it. You may ask to have it run through a meat cubing machine at the market. Or take a tip from the Cayman Islands, where they do it the easy way — with meat tenderizer.

Fried Conch

Tenderize four conchs and cut into thin slices. Dip in flour then beaten egg, then white corn meal. Deep-fat fry by dropping into 375°F fat for 3 minutes, or until browned and slightly crisp. Drain; sprinkle with paprika, a dash of cayenne pepper, and if desired, salt and pepper. Serves 4.

Key West Conch Fritters

1 pound conch
1 egg
1/3 cup milk
1 1/3 cups sifted flour
2 tsp. baking powder
1/2 tsp. salt
1 Tbsp. onion, minced
2 small hot peppers, chopped fine

Put conch through food grinder, using coarse blade, or pound conch and cut into tiny pieces. Beat egg, and combine with milk. Sift flour with baking powder and salt. Add to egg mixture. Add chopped conch, onion, and chopped peppers.

Drop by spoonfuls into hot (375°F) fat; brown on all sides. Drain on paper towels. Serve hot with tartar sauce or cocktail sauce for dunking.

(Note: To reduce the hot pepper taste, reduce the amount of hot peppers, or just use a dash of hot pepper sauce instead.) **Makes 3 dozen.**

Peppery Conch Salad

1 pound cleaned, dressed conch
Key lime juice
1 large onion, chopped fine
1 cup celery, diced
2 medium pickled hot peppers, chopped fine
1 medium tomato, chopped
1 cup chopped lettuce
½ tsp. salt

Cut conch into strips about ¼ inch wide and 1 inch long. Place in bowl; cover with lime juice. Chill 4 to 5 hours. Drain off lime juice; cover conch with more lime juice. Chill 5 hours longer. Drain conch; combine with onion, celery, hot peppers, tomato, lettuce and salt. Toss lightly. Serve with mayonnaise. **Serves 6.**

Corn Meal Conch Fritters

1¾ cups water-ground corn meal
4 Tbsp. flour
1½ tsp. salt
3 tsp. baking powder
1¾ cups milk
2 hot pickled peppers, chopped fine
2 eggs, slightly beaten
¾ pound conch, coarsely ground
1 small onion, minced

In a bowl, mix corn meal, flour, salt and baking powder. Add milk, peppers and eggs. Stir to blend. Put conch through food grinder using coarse blade, or pound with a mallet. Cut into very small pieces. Add conch and onion to corn meal mixture and blend.

Drop spoonfuls of batter into 375°F fat. Make batter thicker or thinner, as desired, by adding more corn meal or milk. Fry until lightly browned on one side; turn and brown on the other side. Drain on paper towels.

(Note: For quick and easy version, start with hushpuppy mix, follow instructions for mixing, and add chopped conch and hot peppers.) **Serves 6.**

Conch Chowder

4 conchs
2 quarts water
¼ pound salt pork, diced
3 large onions, diced
1 cup celery, diced
1 cup carrot, diced
2 large green peppers, diced
2 large tomatoes, peeled, diced
2 med. potatoes, peeled, diced
2 Tbsp. flour
½ tsp. thyme
1½ tsp. salt
1 tsp. garlic salt
¼ tsp. pepper
2 pickled hot peppers, chopped fine, OR 2 dashes liquid hot pepper sauce

Pound conchs with meat mallet or plate to soften tough tissues. Boil in salted water until tender, 30 minutes or more. Remove conch and dice, saving broth.

Fry salt pork. Add onions, celery, carrot, green pepper, tomatoes. Sauté until tender but not browned. Add potatoes, stir in flour. Add broth, diced conch, thyme, salts, pepper, hot peppers. Simmer about 15 minutes or until potatoes are tender. If desired, place a teaspoonful of sherry in each bowl, before pouring in conch chowder. **Serves 4 to 6.**

Cook's Tip: *If a friend brings you a live conch, don't panic. Scrub the shell under cold running water. Cover with boiling water in a heavy pot. Add 1 tablespoon salt and juice of a lemon. Cover, bring back to a boil, and boil 3 minutes. Drain and cool. Pry out the meat, cut off the black foot and curly tip. Rinse and tenderize.*

Crab

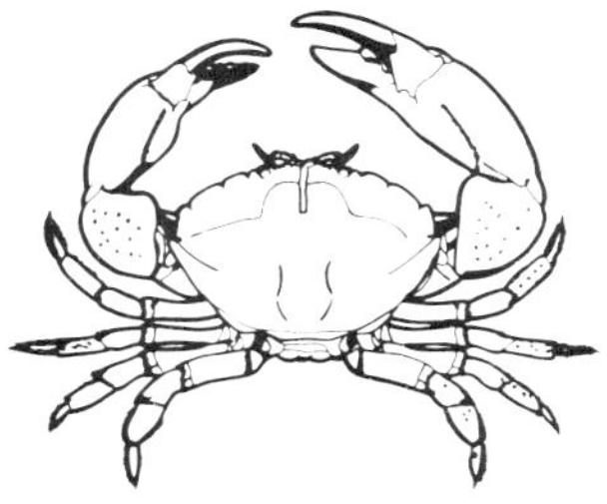

King of the seafood realm is the stone crab, a delicacy more expensive than steak and every bit as delicious. Seafood restaurants feature stone crabs, but they can be hard to find at the market. Stone crabs are in season from mid-October to mid-May, and may not be taken at any other time.

The claw is the only part of the stone crab which is eaten; each crab has two claws. It is illegal to strip the crab of both of its claws, because, when thrown back into the water, he can't feed himself without a claw. If he survives, the crab's missing claw will re-grow, and provide more crab meat in the future.

Blue crabs are Florida's most plentiful crabs, but you may find it difficult to buy fresh ones. They are in season from April through October. Blue crab is sold as lump meat (white meat from the front of the crab's body) and flake meat (small pieces from the rear and center). Claw meat is brownish in color and is used in casseroles or mixed dishes, while the white meat is preferred in cocktails and salads.

Soft-shell crabs are crabs which have shed their outer covering just prior to being caught, so recently that their new shells have not yet hardened.

Boiled Hard Shell Crabs

Bring to boil a large pot of water, adding one tablespoon salt for each quart. With tongs, slide thoroughly washed hard shell crabs into the boiling water, one at a time. Immediately reduce heat; simmer 25 minutes, until crabs turn a bright orange color. With tongs, place cooked crabs upside down in another pot filled with boiling water, and hold until bubbles stop rising.

Wash, drain and cool crabs. Under cold running water, slip fingers under top shell; pull pointed apron at base away from the body, being careful not to break the top shell (save it, for use in baking). Slowly twist and pull, so that the apron (the small piece at the back of the shell which ends in a point) and intestinal vein come out together. Discard both. Scrub crab under cold running water. Holding legs, pull chest section free. Cut out and discard feathery lung sections at top. Remove and save liver (tomalley).

With a hammer, crack shells and remove the meat with a nut pick. Be careful to remove all shell portions. Use meat in salads or other recipes, or serve crabmeat with warm melted butter.

Boiled Soft Shell Crabs

(Note: Since most of the soft shell crab is edible – including the shell – it is usually broiled or breaded and fried, or deep-fat fried.)

Stick a sharp knife into the body between the eyes to kill the live crab. Wash in several changes of water. Lift back the tapering points on each side of the back shell; remove the spongy substance (gills and sandbags) under them. Turn the crab on its back; with a knife, remove the apron, following method given above.

Roll crabs in a mixture of ¼ cup butter, two tablespoons lemon juice, and a couple of drops of red hot sauce. Roll them in flour. Place on broiler rack two inches below heat, and broil for about 10 minutes, turning once. Allow two crabs per serving.

Crab Bisque

1 pound blue crab meat, fresh or pasteurized
2 Tbsp. onion, finely chopped
2 Tbsp. celery, finely chopped
¼ cup melted butter or margarine
3 Tbsp. all-purpose flour
1 tsp. salt
¼ tsp. paprika
dash white pepper
1 quart milk
¼ cup chopped parsley

Carefully pick out any pieces of shell or cartilage from crabmeat. Sauté celery and onion in butter until tender but not brown. Blend in flour and seasonings. Gradually add milk, stirring constantly; cook until thick. Add crabmeat; heat. Just before serving, sprinkle with parsley. **Serves 6.**

Crab Cocktail Salad

1 cup chili sauce
1 Tbsp. prepared horseradish
1-2 Tbsp. lime juice
⅛ tsp. garlic powder OR
small clove garlic, crushed
⅛ tsp. dried dill
½ cup sauterne or rosé wine
1½ tsp. instant minced onion OR
2 Tbsp. chopped green onion
1 pound crabmeat
crisp romaine or lettuce
hard-cooked egg slices
ripe olives

Combine chili sauce, horseradish, lime juice, garlic, dill, wine and onion. Refrigerate several hours or overnight in a closed container. Add half of crabmeat to sauce. Arrange romaine on plates; top with remaining crabmeat. Spoon on the crabmeat sauce. Garnish with egg slices and olives. (Note: for a creamy or Louis-type dressing, add ½ cup mayonnaise or dairy sour cream before refrigerating.) **Serves 6.**

Stone Crabs

If you buy stone crabs already cooked, you may serve them immediately or freeze them. But if you catch your own, you must cook the crab claws the day they are caught. Only cooked meat is used in recipes.

To cook the claws, first wash them thoroughly. Heat a big pot of water to a boil, add salt, and boil claws 15 minutes, uncovered, over medium heat. Lift the claws out with tongs and drop them at once into a pot of icy cold water. Cover with ice and leave two minutes. This prevents the meat from sticking to the shell. Cool, dry thoroughly, and place claws in freezer bags. Mark date frozen, and keep no longer than three months.

To remove meat from the claws, crack them with a hammer and pick it out. Stone crab claws are excellent served hot with

Cook's Tip: *There is no waste in crabmeat. One pound serves four people well. Fishermen and gourmets prefer their soft-shell crabs and delicately-flavored stone crabs freshly caught, cooked and picked from the shell. But for quick, easy preparation, look for crabmeat in half- and one-pound tins. The leg meat is great for salads and deviled crab. Or get the frozen giant crab legs from Alaska and broil them.*

melted butter, or cold with mustard sauce. For a gift with real Florida flavor, there's nothing better than a chilled jar of pickled stone crab claws. Here's how to make them:

Pickled Stone Crab Claws

2½ pounds stone crab claws, fresh or frozen
2 medium onions, sliced
2 cups vegetable oil
2 cups white vinegar
¾ cup sugar
⅓ cup capers with juice
2 tsp. salt
2 tsp. celery seed

Thaw stone crab claws, if frozen. Crack and remove outer shell, leaving meat attached to one side of claw. Make alternate layers of crab claws and onion rings in sealable container. Mix remaining ingredients; pour over crab claws and onions. Seal; place in refrigerator for 6 hours or more, shaking or inverting container occasionally. Remove stone crab claws from marinade and serve. **Serves 6.**

Chilled, Pickled Stone Crab Claws are sure to win raves.

Southern Deviled Crab

- ½ cup onion, finely chopped
- ¼ cup green pepper, finely chopped
- 3 Tbsp. butter or margarine
- 3 Tbsp. flour
- 1½ cups light cream
- 2 egg yolks, beaten slightly
- dash red hot sauce
- ½ tsp. salt
- 2 tsp. Worcestershire sauce
- 1 tsp. dry mustard
- 2 cups crabmeat, drained, boned and flaked OR
  2 7½-oz. cans crabmeat
- 1 cup buttered bread crumbs (2 slices)
- 2 Tbsp. melted butter or margarine

Heat oven to 375°F. Pick out all pieces of shell and cartilage from crabmeat. Sauté onion and green pepper in 3 tablespoons butter until tender but not brown. Add flour; mix until smooth. Gradually stir in cream. Cook in double boiler over hot water, stirring constantly until sauce thickens. Stir a small amount of hot sauce into slightly beaten egg yolks; add to sauce remaining in the pan. Heat 2 minutes. Remove from heat; add hot sauce, salt, Worcestershire, mustard, and mix well. Stir in crab meat. Spoon crab mixture into 6 buttered ramekins or a one-quart casserole. Pour melted butter over bread crumbs; sprinkle on crab mixture. Bake in 375°F oven for 25 minutes or until golden brown. **Serves 6.**

Do-Ahead Crab Soufflé

- 4 slices white bread, cubed
- 2 cups flaked crabmeat (fresh, frozen or canned)
- ½ cup mayonnaise
- 1 medium onion, chopped
- 1 cup celery, chopped
- 1 medium green pepper, chopped
- 6 slices white bread
- 4 eggs
- 3 cups milk
- 1 can condensed cream of mushroom soup
- ¾ cup shredded Cheddar cheese
- paprika

Grease 7- x 11-inch baking dish and cover bottom evenly with bread cubes. Combine crabmeat, mayonnaise, onion, celery, green pepper; spoon over bread cubes. Trim crusts from remaining bread slices; arrange over crabmeat mixture to cover. Beat together eggs and milk; pour over bread. Cover; chill in refrigerator 8 hours or longer. At serving time, heat oven to 325°F; remove cover and bake souffle for 15 minutes. Spread soup evenly over bread slices and top with shredded cheese. Sprinkle with paprika. Bake 1 hour longer. **Serves 12.**

Crabber's Creation

(Both economical and elegant!)

- **1 pound blue crab meat, fresh, frozen or pasteurized**
- **1 7-oz. pkg. long grain and wild rice**
- **2 cups fresh mushrooms, sliced**
- **⅓ cup olive oil or vegetable oil**
- **1 tsp. salt**
- **½ tsp. white pepper**
- **2 Tbsp. extra dry vermouth**
- **2 Tbsp. lemon or lime juice**

Remove any shell or cartilage from crab meat. Cook rice according to package directions. Add fresh mushrooms 5 minutes before end of cooking time. Preheat electric skillet to 325°F, then add oil, salt and pepper. Stir in crab meat, vermouth and lemon juice. Cook 2 to 3 minutes, stirring frequently until crabmeat is thoroughly heated. Serve immediately over wild rice mixture. **Serves 6.**

Lobster

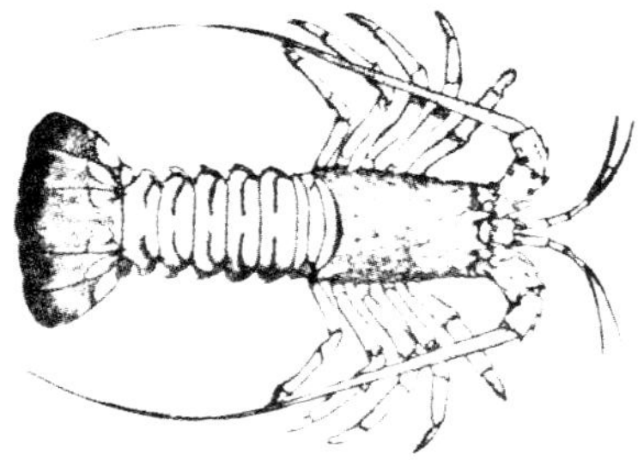

Florida lobster was once so plentiful in the Florida Keys that it was common, everyday fare and early settlers were embarrassed when they had to serve it to guests. Those were the good old days!

Florida's own lobster is called by various names — spiny lobster, rock lobster, or crawfish — and thrives along the coasts, but especially among the reefs off the Florida Keys. It is a cousin of the well-known Maine lobster, but unlike its Maine relative, the spiny lobster has no claws, has antennae growing from the head, and has most of its meat in its tail.

Unless you're lucky enough to trap your own, you will have to settle for fresh-cooked or cooked and frozen spiny lobster, because they are not sold live, as Maine lobsters are.

Whatever method you choose to cook the delicious meat, be very careful not to overcook it, or it will toughen. And do pull on kitchen gloves to handle live lobster. Those sharp-edged shells can hurt your fingers!

Lobster Tails

Yes, it's true. Lobster meat tastes sweet and more delicious when cooked live. But precooked or frozen lobster is quicker and easier to prepare. The choice is yours.

Most spiny lobsters are taken in South African or Australian waters, and labeled "rock lobster tails." They are frozen uncooked and should be thawed thoroughly in the refrigerator or under cold running water, unless the recipe states otherwise. Then they may be boiled, broiled, stuffed or served with a flavored butter such as garlic butter. Plan to refrigerate and use lobster meat in no more than three days. When you buy cooked lobster, be sure the tail curls up and never droops. A curled-up tail shows that the lobster was cooked while alive.

Live Spiny Lobsters

Before you venture out to catch your own lobsters, check with the Marine Patrol on regulations such as season and number limits. Poaching or illegal catches can result in heavy penalties, so play it safe and check first. When you do get a spiny lobster, most people would recommend boiling it, then splitting and cleaning it for broiling or baking. Watch the time you spend on the second cooking, though. Keep it to an absolute minimum. Just heat it through, no more! Overcooking makes the meat rubbery.

Once cooked, cut off the legs and antennae. Use a sharp, heavy knife to split the lobster down the back. Dig out the stomach from the body section and the intestinal vein running from stomach to the tip of the tail. If you're fortunate enough to get a female full of coral roe, mix this with the green liver, called tomalley, and you have a delectable treat! Every part of lobster is edible, except for the shell. Cut around the shell to loosen the meat and lift it out with a fork.

Live Maine Lobster

When you buy, look for a lively lobster. Most people prefer to kill the lobster by plunging it into a big pot of boiling salted water — except New England purists, who insist on steaming it. A helpful tip: the meat will stay more tender if, before boiling, you place the live lobster on ice for an hour.

Before it is baked or broiled, the lobster must be killed, then split and cleaned. You can kill it by placing it on a wooden board, stomach side down, and using a sharp knife, cutting through the spot where the tail and body sections meet. The creature dies at once because the spinal cord is cut. Never mind if it thrashes around a bit afterward. That's just muscle reflex. If this troubles you, some markets will boil the lobster for you, even split and clean it. Check it out in your area.

How to Boil Lobster

Boiling is a popular method, but arguments rage over the best liquid to use — from plain, salted water, sea water, beer or ale, to water seasoned with garlic, bay leaf, lime juice and red pepper. Taste test to find your favorite.

Boiled Lobster

To boil two lobsters, heat 6 quarts of salted water to a rolling boil and plunge the lobsters in, head first. Cover loosely. After water returns to a boil, boil 4 minutes, then reduce heat to simmer and cook about 25 minutes. Lobster will turn a bright red. With tongs, lift out lobster. Place it on its back and cut it in half lengthwise. Remove dark vein and sac near the head and discard. Loosen meat around the edges and serve hot with plenty of butter; if desired, crack claws before serving. Garnish with Florida lime wedges.

Steamed Lobster

Use only small lobsters, from 1⅛ pounds to 1½ pounds. Place lobsters on a rack in a large steamer pan with 2 to 4 cups boiling water under the rack. Cover tightly. Important — if top is loose, slip a sheet of foil between pan and cover, and fasten tightly. Bring to a boil, keeping heat high, and steam 6 to 8 minutes. (Tip: You'll get an even greater taste if you use sea water, and add a bit of seaweed to the pot.)

If lobster is for a cold dish, chill in refrigerator before removing meat from the shell.

Japanese Steamed Rock Lobster

- **3 8-oz. packages frozen rock lobster tails**
- **6 mushrooms, sliced**
- **6 scallions, cut into long, thin strips**
- **1 cup celery, thinly sliced**
- **1 bunch broccoli, trimmed and cut into flowerets**
- **1 Tbsp. soy sauce**
- **1 envelope dehydrated chicken broth**
- **¼ cup water**

With scissors, remove thin underside membrane from lobster tails. Push a bamboo skewer lengthwise through tail, to prevent curling. Place a colander over an inch or so of boiling water in a large pot, or use a steamer basket. Put rock lobster tails into colander. Place vegetables on top and around lobster. Mix soy sauce, broth and water; brush onto tails and vegetables. Cover pot; steam 20 minutes or until vegetables are crisp-tender and tail meat has lost its translucency and is opaque. Serve hot with fried rice. **Serves 6.**

Lobster Boiled in Beer

2 packages frozen lobster tails
2 cans beer
2 cloves garlic, chopped
1 tsp. thyme
2 Tbsp. chopped chives
2 Tbsp. chopped parsley
2 bay leaves
1 Tbsp. dry mustard
1 Tbsp. salt
½ tsp. black pepper
juice of 1 lemon

Thaw lobster thoroughly, under running water or in the refrigerator. Place beer and seasonings in large saucepan; bring to boil. Add lobster. Return to boil, then reduce heat and simmer 10 to 12 minutes. If necessary, add water or additional beer to cover lobster tails. Remove from cooking liquid. Before serving, split lobster tails by cutting lengthwise through thin undershell. Serve hot with lemon wedges and melted butter, or cold with a seafood salad dressing. **Serves 2.**

Neptune's Newburg

¾ pound cooked lobster meat
¼ cup butter or margarine
2 Tbsp. flour
1 tsp. salt
¼ tsp. paprika
dash cayenne pepper
1 pint Half-and-Half
2 egg yolks, beaten
2 Tbsp. dry sherry or Madeira
crisp toast

Cut lobster meat into ½-inch pieces. Melt butter; blend in flour and seasonings. Add cream gradually and cook until thick and smooth, stirring constantly. Stir a little hot sauce into egg yolk; add to remaining sauce, stirring constantly. Add lobster meat; heat. Remove from heat and slowly stir in wine. Serve immediately on toast triangles. **Serves 6.**

Crunchy Lobster Salad

2 cups flaked lobster, fresh cooked or canned
3 Tbsp. French dressing
1 cup chopped celery
2 Tbsp. chopped sweet pickle
2 Tbsp. chopped onion
2 hard cooked eggs, chopped
½ tsp. salt
dash freshly ground pepper
½ cup mayonnaise or salad dressing
a few capers
lettuce

Remove any shell from lobster, or drain canned lobster. Combine lobster, dressing, celery, pickle, onion, eggs, salt, pepper. Be careful not to cut lobster into pieces that are too small. Chill. Drain; serve on bed of lettuce, garnished with mayonnaise, capers. (Also tastes great served in cantaloupe or avocado halves.) **Serves 6.**

Lettuce-Baked Lobster Tails

6 ½-pound lobster tails, fresh or frozen
1 cup margarine or butter, melted, divided in half
¼-½ tsp. garlic powder
½ tsp. salt
paprika
10-12 lettuce leaves, rinsed and drained

Thaw lobster if frozen. Fan cut lobster tails by cutting off the undershell, leaving tail fan and upper shell in place. Place lobster shell side down on baking sheet. Add garlic powder and salt to ½ cup margarine and brush onto lobster meat; sprinkle with paprika. Cover tails completely with damp lettuce leaves; bake at 400°F for 15-20 minutes or until lobster meat is opaque white and tender. Discard lettuce leaves. Serve with remaining melted margarine. **Serves 6.**

Broiled Lobster with Parsley Sauce

2 live lobsters (1 pound each)
1 Tbsp. melted butter or margarine
¼ tsp. salt
dash white pepper
dash paprika
Parsley Sauce (recipe below)

Follow instructions given under "Live Spiny Lobsters" for killing and cleaning lobster. If you are using Maine lobsters, crack the claws. Lay lobsters open as flat as possible on a broiler pan. Brush with butter; sprinkle with salt, pepper, and paprika. Broil 4 inches from source of heat 15 to 20 minutes, or until lightly browned. During last 5 minutes of cooking, brush lobster meat with Parsley Sauce. (You may choose not to use Parsley Sauce, and serve instead with ¼ cup melted butter and 1 tablespoon lemon juice.) **Serves 2.**

Parsley Sauce

⅔ cup olive oil or cooking oil
⅓ cup wine vinegar
1 tsp. thyme
½ tsp. salt
¼ tsp. white pepper
1 Tbsp. chopped parsley
1 clove garlic, chopped very fine

Mix ingredients together and heat to a boil. Simmer 5 minutes and then keep warm. Brush broiling lobsters with sauce. (Note: Cover and refrigerate any leftover sauce to use later — or, recipe may be cut in half.) **Serves 6.**

A beautiful dish with heavenly taste — Herbed Lobster Thermidor.

Herbed Lobster Thermidor

- 6 Florida lobster (spiny lobster), OR
  6 frozen rock lobster tails, OR
  3⅔ cups cooked lobster meat
- 3 Tbsp. butter or margarine
- 2 Tbsp. flour
- 1 cup light cream
- ½ tsp. poultry seasoning
- ¼ tsp. powdered dry mustard
- ⅛ tsp. ground black pepper
- ½ tsp. paprika
- 1 tsp. salt
- 1 Tbsp. instant minced onion
- 2 Tbsp. dry sherry
- ¼ cup grated Parmesan cheese

Cook lobster using instructions on page 83, or follow those shown on frozen lobster package. Remove meat; cut into chunks. Melt butter or margarine in heavy pan. Blend in flour. Stir in cream and cook, stirring constantly, until mixture thickens somewhat. Add seasonings, instant minced onion, sherry and the lobster, saving a few large chunks for the top of the casserole. Use the mixture to fill lobster shells, or turn into 6 individual buttered baking dishes or a one-quart casserole. Put reserved lobster chunks on top; sprinkle with Parmesan cheese. For shells, place under broiler to brown (about 3 minutes); for casserole, brown in preheated 450°F oven. Sprinkle with paprika and serve hot. **Serves 6.**

Creole Crawfish Étouffée

2 sticks butter or margarine
½ cup finely chopped green pepper
1 cup finely chopped onion
½ cup finely chopped celery
1 cup finely chopped green onions
1 tsp. minced garlic
2 Tbsp. flour
1 cup canned, whole, peeled tomatoes
2 cups fish stock
2 tsp. salt
1 tsp. black pepper
dash red hot sauce, OR
¼ tsp. ground red pepper
1 Tbsp. Worcestershire sauce
1½ cups crawfish (lobster) meat

Melt butter in heavy skillet (the Creoles use iron skillets). Sauté green pepper, onion, celery and green onions. Simmer 10 to 15 minutes until tender. Add tomatoes and minced garlic; continue cooking 1 minute. Stir flour into 1 tablespoon cold water then add to vegetables and stir constantly until golden brown. Blend in fish stock; simmer 10 minutes. Add salt, pepper, hot sauce or red pepper (Creoles add enough to make it tingly hot), Worcestershire and lobster meat. Cook slowly 15 to 20 minutes, stirring to prevent sticking. Remove from heat and let stand 30 minutes to let flavors blend. Reheat and serve over rice. **Serves 4.**

Mussels

The crescent-shaped mussel is an old Indian favorite, and one of the most nutritious and delicious of all seafoods. In Europe, it's regarded as the poor man's oyster.

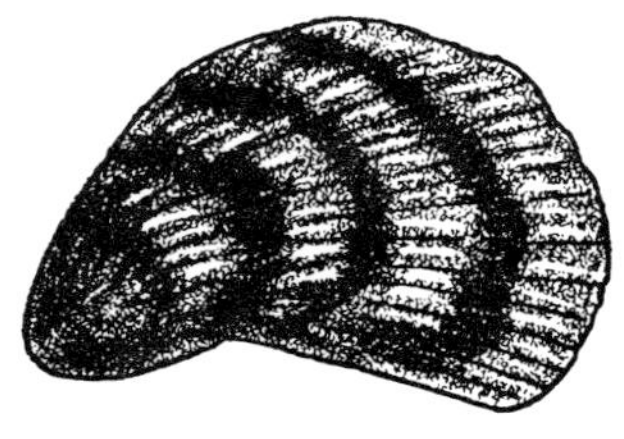

Many varieties are found along both U.S. coasts. In Florida, mussels abound along the coasts, and in the broad estuaries of our many rivers. Floridians enjoy searching for mussels at low tide, using a screwdriver to pry them off rocks. It is always wise to be sure that the waters are not polluted. Mussels can be gathered year round, but the best times are in spring and in late summer.

Any mussel that is open or has black mud in the shell should be discarded, *never* eaten. When shopping for mussels, whether the shells are rough or have been cleaned, it's wise to buy a larger number than needed. Usually, many shells will be open, cracked, broken, or filled with mud, and these must of course be rejected.

How to Clean Mussels

Remove the hair-like beard and scrape crusted matter from the outside of the shell with a sharp knife. Using a wire brush, scrub the shells thoroughly under plenty of cold running water. Test each one by rubbing briskly with the fingers. If any substance oozes out of the shell, discard it! Also reject any slightly open shells that don't snap shut as you handle them.

Next, drop the mussels into a deep pan filled with cold, fresh water, and soak them for an hour or two so that they will throw off any sand or salt. When ready to drain, do not pour off the water. Just scoop out the mussels, leaving the sand at the bottom. In a clean pan, wash until the water runs clear.

Steaming Mussels

Steaming is the easiest way to open the shells. Pour a half-inch of water into a large, heavy pot, add the mussels, cover and steam over high heat, shaking the pot frequently until the shells open — about 8 minutes.

If the broth is to be used in a soup or stew, let the pot of steamed mussels sit for several minutes. Then very carefully drain off the liquid through three layers of cheesecloth, to eliminate any sand.

To serve, ladle mussels in their shells into soup bowls and set out bowls of plain or garlic butter for dipping, with parsley-sprinkled lemon wedges. Provide plenty of big napkins, and paper bibs if you have them. Mussel lovers like to scoop the tasty meat from the shell with another shell, using it as a spoon.

Italian Mussel Salad

2½ pounds small mussels, cleaned and debearded
½ cup wine vinegar, divided
¼ tsp. dried thyme
6 peppercorns
1 bay leaf
½ cup minced Vidalia onion
¼ cup chopped parsley
½ cup vegetable or olive oil
fresh watercress greens

In a large pot, place ¼ cup vinegar, thyme, peppercorns and bay leaf. Add mussels and cover; steam until shells open, about 8 minutes. Remove mussels with slotted spoon and discard broth. Remove mussels from shells, trim out dark sections and drain on paper towels. Place still-warm mussels in large bowl.

Combine minced onion, parsley, oil and remaining ¼ cup vinegar. Pour over mussels and toss. Season to taste with salt and pepper. Chill well and serve on a bed of crisp watercress. (This salad looks pretty served in shell-shaped salad dishes, garnished with black olives.) **Serves 4 to 6.**

Cook's Tip:

To add flavor to steamed mussels, add to the cooking water a small bunch of tied-up parsley, finely chopped onion, thyme, bay leaf and — if you like — a generous splash of dry white wine. Of course, the cooking broth is to be strained before it is used in a seafood dish.

Cook mussels this way, then serve in soup plates, covered with the strained broth and sprinkled with chopped parsley, and you have the delightful French dish Moules Mariniere.

Bacon Baked Oysters (page 94) are hot and juicy, flavored with Parmesan cheese.

Oysters

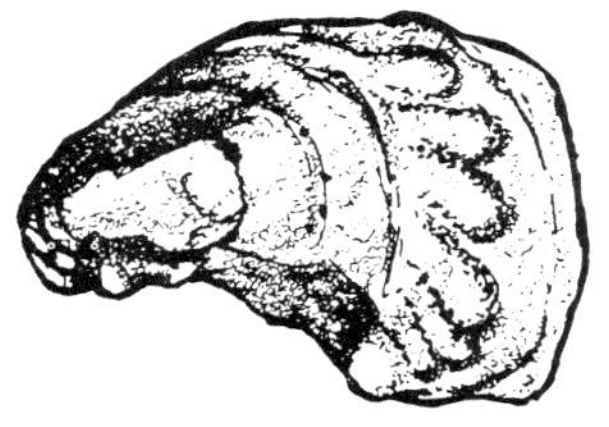

Oysters normally grow in shallow, brackish, warm bays. They vary in size, texture and flavor according to the species and where they are harvested. Floridians usually eat Eastern oysters, which are found along the coasts of Texas, Louisiana, and in great quantity along the northwest coast of Florida and at Cape Canaveral. These Atlantic oysters are generally mild and soft, with an earthy flavor. Moving north, oysters are harvested in Maryland, Virginia, New England and Nova Scotia — these taste more crisp and salty.

Eastern oysters are sold live in the shell, fresh, shucked or canned. When buying live oysters in shells, be sure the shells are tightly closed. If not, *don't eat them!* Live oysters in the shell can be covered with damp cloths and kept in a cool place for up to 24 hours. For best taste, eat shucked oysters the day they are bought – if fresh, they can be wrapped airtight and frozen at 0°F for up to four months. Thaw them in the refrigerator (not at room temperature) and once they're thawed, never refreeze them.

How to cook oysters? As little as possible! Use low temperatures and cook just until they plump up and the edges curl. If you overcook oysters, they get tough and rubbery. Read about oysters in the Nutritional Fish Facts chapter for important information: these succulent bivalves are rich in vitamins and minerals, and contain more phosphorus (a "brain food") than any other food!

How to Open and Clean Oysters

First, put on thick cotton gloves to protect your hands. Under cold running water, scrub the shells well with a stiff-bristled brush, then drain. Place oyster on a table, flat shell up, holding it with your left hand. Use an oyster knife in your right hand to force the shells open at or near the thin end. To make it easier to insert the knife, use a hammer to break off the thin end, or "bill." Follow the bottom contour of the shell and cut the large muscle close to the flat upper shell to which it is attached. Remove the shell, being careful to save the liquid.

Cut the lower end of the same muscle attached to the deep half of the shell. Before serving, check carefully for bits of shell. Serve raw from the shell, or use the shucked oysters in cooking.

How to Poach Oysters

When a recipe calls for cooked or fried oysters, it's wise to poach them first. This removes their slippery coating, and makes them taste great in cocktails, salads and other dishes. Remove oysters from their shells and carefully pour the oyster liquid into a saucepan. Bring to a boil, slip oysters into hot liquid and immediately reduce to simmer. Simmer about 4 minutes or until oysters are slightly firm and plump and edges curl. Drain; use in hot dishes, or cover and chill for cold dishes.

Cook's Tip: *To preserve their liquid, always store oysters with the rounded shell down. Many people prefer not to use salt with oysters, finding them salty enough. Experiment to see if you agree.*

Super Scalloped Oysters

1 cup coarse cracker crumbs
¼ cup melted butter or margarine
2 dozen shucked oysters, drained
¼ cup oyster liquid
¼ tsp. salt
⅛ tsp. pepper
½ cup light cream
1 tsp. Worcestershire sauce
2 Tbsp. dry white wine
dash cayenne pepper

Heat oven to 400°F. Combine crumbs and butter. Cover bottom of 10 x 6 x 2-inch baking dish with a third of the crumb mixture. Look oysters over carefully and remove any bits of shell, then chop coarsely. Arrange half of the oysters on top of crumbs. Combine oyster liquid with salt, pepper, cream, Worcestershire, wine and cayenne pepper. Spoon half of this sauce over oysters in pan. Sprinkle on half of the remaining crumbs, top with the rest of the oysters, then the remaining sauce, then the remaining crumbs. Bake at 400°F for 30 minutes or until set. Serve hot. **Serves 4.**

Fried Oysters

1 pint large, fresh oysters
1/3 cup flour
1 tsp. salt
1/8 tsp. freshly ground pepper
1 egg
1 Tbsp. water
2/3 cup cracker or bread crumbs
1/4 cup vegetable or olive oil
1 Tbsp. butter

Carefully lay oysters on colander to dry. With a soft cloth, dry quickly and gently, handling as little as possible. Mix together flour, salt and pepper. Beat egg with water. Dip oysters in flour mixture, then in egg, then in crumbs. In a not-too-deep saucepan, heat oil until smoking hot and add butter (to help oysters turn crisp and brown). Put in only enough oysters to cover the bottom of the pan; brown on one side and then turn, cooking about 5 minutes on each side. Serve at once with lemon wedges sprinkled with parsley. **Serves 4.**

Broiled Oysters

4 slices dry toast
2 dozen oysters
8 Tbsp. melted butter
1/2 tsp. garlic salt
1/2 tsp. seasoned salt
paprika

Cut toast into triangles, removing edges if you wish. Place several toast triangles in each of 4 individual shallow casseroles. Place 6 oysters in each casserole, on top of toast. Pour 2 tablespoons melted butter over oysters in each dish. Add salt, reducing amounts to suit your taste. (Be sure casseroles are broiler-proof.)

In preheated broiler, broil about 4 minutes, just until edges of oysters curl. Watch carefully — overcooking will make oysters shrink and toughen. Remove from broiler, sprinkle with paprika, and serve with remaining toast triangles arranged around the casseroles. **Serves 4.**

Oyster Omelet

1 pint raw oysters, well drained
1 Tbsp. butter or margarine
6 eggs
1/4 cup light cream
1/4 tsp. salt
1/8 tsp. pepper

Drain oysters; cut into small pieces. Over low heat, sauté oysters in butter or margarine until edges curl. Mix together eggs, cream, salt and pepper to taste. Beat with a fork. Pour over oysters in frying pan and scramble lightly. Serve hot. **Serves 4.**

Bacon Baked Oysters

24 fresh oysters, shucked, with curved half-shells saved
6 slices bacon, cut in 1-inch pieces
½ cup mayonnaise
1 cup buttery cracker crumbs, crushed
2 Tbsp. dehydrated chives
1 tsp. Tabasco
½ tsp. Dijon mustard
1 tsp. lemon juice
rock salt
¼ cup Parmesan cheese, grated

In 10-inch frying pan, cook bacon until limp. Set aside. In small bowl, combine remaining ingredients except Parmesan cheese; mix well. Pour a half-inch of coarse rock salt into baking pan. Arrange oysters on salt, each in its half shell, so that they rest firmly. (This is done to prevent them from tipping and spilling their golden contents.) Top each oyster with crumb mixture. Sprinkle with Parmesan cheese and top with bacon pieces. Bake in 400°F oven for 8 to 10 minutes, or just until the edges begin to curl. Be careful not to overcook! **Serves 4 to 6.**

Oysters Rockefeller

36 medium, in-the-shell oysters
4 Tbsp. (½ stick) melted butter
½ cup dry bread crumbs
3 Tbsp. dry white wine
2 Tbsp. chopped, cooked bacon
1 Tbsp. minced parsley
1 tsp. seasoned salt
2 cups cooked spinach, well drained, OR 1½ cups canned or frozen spinach, cooked
¼ cup chopped onion
few drops red hot sauce
rock salt

Heat oven to 450°F. Cook bacon and drain on paper towels. Shuck oysters and rinse well, leaving each in a curved shell for cooking. Refrigerate oysters. Melt butter; combine with bread crumbs. In another bowl, combine wine, bacon, parsley, salt, spinach, onion, and hot sauce. Top each oyster with a spoonful of the spinach mixture, and then sprinkle it with buttered bread crumbs.

Place a layer of rock salt in shallow baking pan or jelly roll pan and carefully set the oysters in the salt. Bake 10 minutes at 450°F or until oysters plump up and edges curl. Slide under broiler for a minute or two until lightly browned. Serve hot with lemon wedges. **Serves 6.**

Oysters Casino

- **1 pint oysters, fresh or frozen**
- **3 slices bacon, chopped**
- **4 Tbsp. onion, chopped**
- **2 Tbsp. green pepper, chopped**
- **2 Tbsp. celery, chopped**
- **1 tsp. lemon or lime juice**
- **½ tsp. salt**
- **½ tsp. Worcestershire sauce**
- **⅛ tsp. pepper**
- **2 drops liquid hot pepper sauce (or more)**

Thaw oysters if frozen. Drain. Remove any remaining pieces of shell particles. Place oysters in well-greased baking dish, about 9 x 9 x 2 inches. Fry bacon until crisp. Add onion, green pepper and celery. Cook until vegetables are tender. Add lemon juice, salt, Worcestershire, pepper and hot sauce; mix well. Spread bacon mixture over oysters. Bake in 350°F oven about 10 minutes or until oysters' edges curl, showing they are done. **Serves 6.**

Cook's Tip:

Remember the old rule about eating oysters only in months containing an "R"? It's no longer true, due to modern methods of refrigerating, freezing and canning, at least in our country. However, that's not true in Europe. Go back to the old rule there, because oysters can taste gritty in the summer and can develop diseases.

With oysters, as with all shellfish, it's wise to buy from clean, well-known markets to be sure you get food harvested from unpolluted waters.

Scallops

The scallop shell figures prominently in world culture, including religion. American Indians used the lovely shell in their dress and rituals. Pilgrims searching for the Holy Grail followed a route leading to the Shrine of St. James in Spain, and used scallop shells as dishes, cups and spoons. Because of this, the shell became the badge of pilgrims, and scallop shells were worn around their necks.

Did you know that many dishes were originally called "scalloped" because they were first served in scallop shells?

Scallops are the only bivalves that swim, and do so by clapping their two round shells together. Like mussels, scallops anchor themselves to rocks as they grow. Scallops up New England way are large — 5 to 7 inches. Southern varieties are smaller and, some say, more tender and sweet. The two varieties are sea scallops (these have a 2-inch or larger "eye" or great muscle, which is the part we eat) and bay scallops (smaller and more delicate, with a creamy pinkish color). Most plentiful in Florida are small, juicy Calico scallops.

Scallops are so perishable that the shells are usually removed aboard the fishing boats, and the delectable muscles are immediately refrigerated or frozen. They are sold shelled, cleaned, fresh or frozen. If frozen, they should be thawed in the refrigerator (*not* at room temperature) and never refrozen.

Large scallops are usually sliced across the grain of the muscle before they are used in recipes. Limit cooking to the least possible time. Overcooking makes scallops tough and dry.

How to Open Scallops

If you're lucky enough to get fresh scallops in the shell, place them in the bottom of a 250°F oven just until the shell pops open. (Of course, you *never* eat a scallop unless its shell is tightly closed.) Cut meat from the shell; trim off the beard and black parts, saving only the white muscle. Rinse well under cold running water and drain.

Scallop Kebobs

- 1 pound sea scallops (about 32)
- 16 small, white onions
- 3 green peppers
- 16 large mushrooms
- 2 Tbsp. lemon or lime juice
- ½ cup melted butter or margarine
- freshly ground pepper
- garlic powder
- paprika
- hot cooked rice

Thaw scallops in refrigerator, if they are frozen. Peel onions and cut peppers in 24 pieces. Remove stems from mushrooms. Cook onions in boiling, salted water for 8 minutes; add pepper pieces and cook 2 minutes longer. Drain. Arrange foods on 8-inch skewers in order: mushroom, pepper, scallop, scallop, onion, pepper, scallop, scallop, onion, pepper, mushroom.

Combine lemon juice and melted butter. Brush skewered food with butter mixture; sprinkle with pepper and garlic powder. Sprinkle scallops with paprika. Broil 2 inches below broiler about 5 minutes, until scallops are tender and lightly browned. Immediately place on a bed of rice, drizzling sauce over kebobs and serving hot.

(Note: Recipe makes 8 kebobs. When kebobs are served as the main entree, plan for 2 skewers per person. Broil 4 kebobs at a time, so that second servings will be hot.) **Serves 4 to 8.**

Wine-Marinated Scallops

- 1½ pounds sea scallops
- ½ cup dry vermouth
- ¼ cup grated fresh ginger, OR candied ginger with sugar removed
- ½ cup olive oil
- 1 clove garlic, crushed
- ½ tsp. salt
- dash pepper
- toast triangles

In bowl, mix together vermouth, ginger, oil, garlic, salt and pepper. Wash scallops under cold running water; drain. Marinate in vermouth mixture, and refrigerate at least 2 hours, preferably more. Preheat broiler. Place scallops in a shallow pan; pour half of marinade over and broil 2 inches from heat 5 to 6 minutes. Halfway through cooking time, turn scallops and baste with remaining marinade. Remove scallops to warm platter, placing them on toast triangles, and pouring the warm sauce over. Serve with tartar sauce. **Serves 6.**

Japanese Tempura with Scallops

- 1 cup all-purpose flour
- ¼ cup cornstarch
- 2 tsp. baking powder
- 2 egg whites
- 1 Tbsp. sesame oil
- 1 tsp. soy sauce
- 1½ cups cold water
- 1 pound sea scallops, sliced
- 2 medium onions, sliced thickly
- 2 zucchini, sliced thickly
- 6 white mushrooms, halved
- 6 summer squash, sliced thickly
- Kikkoman soy sauce
- vegetable oil for frying

Make batter by placing flour, cornstarch and baking powder in large bowl and mixing well. Add egg whites, sesame oil, soy sauce and water; beat until well mixed. Place mixture in refrigerator, covered, for 45 minutes. Cover bottom of wok or electric frying pan with 2 inches of oil and heat to 375°F.

Take batter from refrigerator; stir once. Dip scallops and vegetables into batter; drop into hot oil a few pieces at a time, so that oil does not get too cool. Fry 5 minutes or until lightly browned. Place fried food in a bowl lined with paper towels; cover to keep warm until all food is fried.

This may be served with hot rice and a bowl of soy sauce for dipping. Good, too, with a dish of Tsukemono (Japanese pickles). **Serves 6.**

Scallops and Macaroni Casserole

- 2 cups uncooked shell macaroni
- 1 pound sea scallops, sliced
- 4 Tbsp. butter or margarine
- 1 clove garlic
- 3 Tbsp. cornstarch
- 2 tsp. salt
- ¼ tsp. pepper
- 2¾ cups milk
- ¼ cup dry white wine
- 2 cups grated sharp Cheddar cheese, divided

Thaw scallops in refrigerator if they are frozen. Cook macaroni according to package directions. Drain and set aside. Meanwhile, melt butter in saucepan. Peel and crush garlic; stir into butter and cook over low heat until transparent and pale yellow. Remove garlic; stir in cornstarch, salt and pepper. Gradually add milk, mixing until smooth. Cook over medium heat until mixture thickens, stirring constantly. Boil 2 minutes, still stirring. Add wine and 1½ cups cheese.

Combine sauce, scallop slices and macaroni. Turn into oiled 2-quart casserole. Sprinkle with remaining ½ cup Cheddar cheese.

Bake in 350°F oven 30 minutes or until lightly browned. Serve hot. Great served with a salad of crisp greens bathed in a brisk vinaigrette dressing. **Serves 4 to 6.**

Poached Scallops

(For use in seafood cocktails, salads, Newburgs or curry.)

Thaw scallops in refrigerator, if they are frozen. Cut large scallops in half, use bay scallops whole. Place them in a saucepan, cover with boiling salted water and immediately reduce heat to simmer. Simmer gently 3 minutes. Never let them boil or they toughen. Remove from the pan, drain well, and chill.

Scallops Oriental

(Makes one pound of scallops serve six people!)

1 pound calico or bay scallops, fresh or frozen
2 Tbsp. lemon or lime juice
2 Tbsp. soy sauce
½ tsp. garlic powder
2 Tbsp. vegetable oil
1 cup broccoli flowerets and stalks, thinly sliced
1 cup fresh mushrooms, thinly sliced
1 cup cauliflower, thinly sliced
½ cup green onions, cut in 1-inch pieces
1 Tbsp. vegetable oil
2½ Tbsp. cornstarch
1 tsp. salt
½ tsp. pepper
¾ cup water
3 cups chow mein noodles

Thaw scallops if frozen. Cut large scallops in half. Combine lemon juice, soy sauce and garlic. Pour over scallops. Let marinate while preparing vegetables. In wok, heat oil and add broccoli, mushrooms, cauliflower and green onions. Stir fry 4 minutes at 300°F. Remove vegetables to warm platter. Add remaining table-spoon of oil to wok, if necessary. Drain scallops, saving the marinade. Place scallops in wok. Stir fry for 1 to 2 minutes or until scallops turn opaque. Add vegetables to scallops in wok. In small bowl, combine cornstarch with salt, pepper, water and saved marinade; mix well. Add to scallop-vegetable mixture and stir only until broth thickens. Serve over chow mein noodles. (Note: If you have no wok, an electric skillet works equally well.) **Serves 4 to 6.**

Shrimp

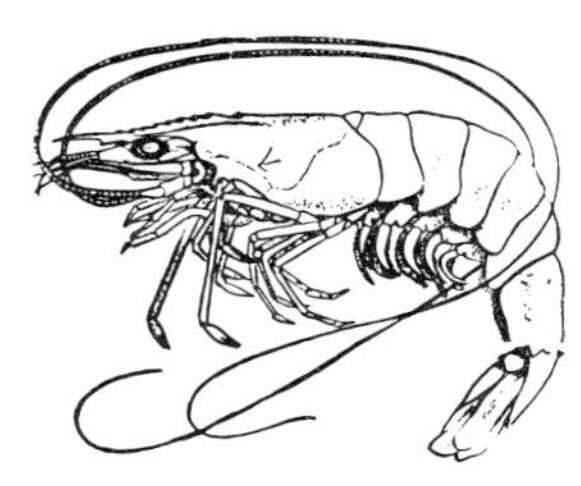

The most popular shellfish in the U.S. is the shrimp. While found all along North American coasts, they are most plentiful from North Carolina to Florida and on into the Gulf of Mexico. While Louisiana waters supply about half the total amount harvested, large numbers are also taken from Florida waters. A recent survey showed that about 600 million pounds of shrimp are consumed by Americans each year. Imported shrimp are included in the total.

Trawlers fish for shrimp, lop off the heads (because they are quickest to spoil) and ice down the remaining tails. The season is year round, but heaviest production is from August through December. That means you can serve delicious Jambalaya, cocktail, scampi, curry or Shrimp Newburg any time you like — and what scrumptious dishes they are!

In years past, the rock shrimp, although found in abundant supply in Mexican and Florida waters, was rejected by commercial fishermen because its very hard shell made it difficult to process. But then along came a machine that could efficiently whip off the shells, and the now the demand for this shrimp has shot up to millions of pounds a year. The rock shrimp meat is firm — somewhat of a cross between shrimp and lobster in taste — and is especially good for broiling.

Shrimp are sold by the pound, the size category based on the number of shrimp per pound. Generally, the groupings are as follows, although they may vary in different areas:

Jumbo: 10–15 per lb.
Large: 26–30 per lb.
Medium: 31–35 per lb.
Tiny Alaskan: 150–180 per lb.

You may buy shrimp fresh, frozen, frozen peeled and breaded, and canned. (When using canned, rinse off the salt before adding to recipe.) While there are several varieties which vary in color from greenish gray to pink to brown when raw, all varieties turn pink or coral-colored when cooked.

When figuring quantities needed, remember that it takes two pounds of raw unshelled shrimp to give you just over a pound of the meat. For most recipes, you will need about a half pound of shrimp meat per person.

Don't hesitate to give shrimp the sniff test before you buy them. They should smell fresh and be firm to the touch. Never buy a package of frozen shrimp that has a broken covering or is covered with ice crystals. It has probably been defrosted and refrozen.

As with all seafood, the same rule applies: cook it quickly so it won't get tough.

No doubt about it — the best of shrimp of all are the ones you catch yourself, and it's not difficult! Take a long-handled net and a lantern, and go out on a chilly night at ebbtide under a full Florida moon. Scoop them up from under a bridge or along a jetty, build a big fire, steam them and douse them in butter. Super!

Boiled Shrimp

(Actually, they're simmered)

2 pounds raw, headless, unpeeled shrimp (fresh or frozen)
5 cups water
2 Tbsp. salt

If shrimp are frozen, thaw them. Peel and devein shrimp. Rinse thoroughly and drain. Add salt to water, bring to a boil. Add shrimp and immediately reduce heat to simmer. Cover and simmer 3 to 4 minutes, or until the largest shrimp is opaque in the center when tested by cutting it in half. Cooking time varies, depending on the size of the shrimp — less for small, a little longer for jumbo size. Drain shrimp. Rinse thoroughly under cold running water for 1 to 2 minutes. Serve warm or well chilled. Yields about 1 pound cooked, peeled, deveined shrimp. Serve over lettuce, topped with your favorite sauce, for shrimp cocktail.

Pickled Shrimp with Pumpernickel

- 1 cup vegetable oil
- 1 cup cider vinegar
- juice of 3 limes or lemons
- 2 Tbsp. sugar
- 5 bay leaves
- 1 tsp. coarsely ground whole black peppercorns
- 1 tsp. dill seeds
- ½ tsp. tarragon leaves
- 1 tsp. celery salt
- 1 tsp. dry mustard
- dash of cayenne pepper
- 6 medium onions, sliced
- 3 pounds shrimp, deveined, cooked and peeled
- 1 small loaf pumpernickel bread, sliced thin

Combine oil, vinegar, lime or lemon juice, sugar, bay leaves, pepper, dill, tarragon, celery salt, mustard and cayenne pepper. Simmer about 10 minutes. Add shrimp; simmer 3 minutes longer. In large china or glass casserole, place layer of sliced onions, layer of shrimp, and repeat until all are used. Pour hot marinade over all; make sure all shrimp are well covered. (If necessary, make more marinade.) Cool slightly, then cover and place in refrigerator. Chill at least 48 hours. Serve cold with sliced pumpernickel. **Serves 6 to 8.**

Avocado Shrimp Salad

- lettuce leaves
- ½ cup small sprigs watercress
- 1 cup chopped celery
- ¼ cup chopped green onions
- 1½ cups cooked, chilled shrimp
- 2 medium tomatoes, cut in wedges
- 5 large stuffed olives, sliced
- ½ grapefruit, peeled and sectioned
- 1 medium avocado, peeled and sliced
- Creamy Seafood Dressing (recipe below)

Pile lettuce leaves lightly in salad bowl. Toss watercress together with celery and onions. Arrange watercress mixture, shrimp, tomatoes, olives, grapefruit and avocado attractively on serving platter. (Note: To keep the avocado green, sprinkle it with a little lime juice.) Place on buffet. Invite each guest to select ingredients from platter for his own salad plate. Serve creamy seafood dressing on the side. **Serves 6.**

Creamy Seafood Dressing

- 1 envelope old-fashioned French salad dressing mix
- ¼ cup mayonnaise
- 2 Tbsp. catsup
- 2 Tbsp. lime or lemon juice

Mix French dressing as according to package directions. Use only ¼ cup of prepared dressing (refrigerate the rest); add dressing to mayonnaise, catsup and lime juice. Stir to blend. Chill well. **Makes ½ cup.**

New Orleans Gumbo

- 1 pound fresh okra, or 1 pkg. frozen)
- 3 strips bacon, OR 3 oz. ham, chopped
- 2 Tbsp. flour
- 2 med. onions, chopped fine
- 1 med. green pepper, chopped
- 1 hot pepper, chopped very fine
- 2 stalks celery, chopped
- 2 cloves garlic, chopped fine
- 1 tsp. thyme
- 1 8-oz. can tomato sauce or paste
- 2 bay leaves
- 1 tsp. parsley flakes, OR 1 Tbsp. fresh parsley, chopped
- 1 quart boiling water
- 2 pounds cleaned, uncooked shrimp
- hot cooked rice

Thaw okra if frozen. Slice and wipe with cloth to prevent it from being slimy, but don't wash it. Fry bacon or ham until halfway done. Add okra; cook slowly, stirring often, until dark brown. Don't let it burn! Add flour, cook and stir until flour is dark brown.

Add onion, green pepper, hot pepper, celery and garlic. Cook until onions are tender. Add thyme, tomato sauce or paste, bay leaves, parsley and boiling water. Bring to boil again; add shrimp, and season to taste with salt and pepper. Simmer about 20 minutes. Serve in large bowls with fluffy white rice.

(Note: For a real Creole touch, use filé — powdered sassafras— as a thickener. If you use the filé, omit the okra and start by browning flour in bacon fat. When gumbo is done, add 2 tablespoons filé, remove from heat, cover and let stand 30 minutes before serving.) **Serves 6.**

Iced Dilly Shrimp Soup

- ½ pound cooked shrimp
- 1 quart buttermilk
- 1½ cups cucumber, peeled and chopped
- ½ cup green onion, chopped
- ½ cup green pepper, seeded, chopped
- 3 stalks celery, sliced
- ½ tsp. salt
- ⅛ tsp. pepper
- 1 Tbsp. chopped fresh dill, OR 1 tsp. dried dillweed
- sour cream (optional)

In a large bowl, combine all ingredients except dill. Cover and place in refrigerator overnight, or for at least 12 hours. Just before serving, add dill and, if you like, a dollop of sour cream. (Note: wonderful in Florida's warm weather, served in a bowl of crushed ice.) **Serves 4 to 6.**

Shrimp with Yellow Rice

(from Tampa's Columbia Restaurant)

½ cup Spanish olive oil
2 cloves garlic, chopped fine
1 small onion, chopped fine
1 green pepper, chopped
1 pound raw shrimp, peeled, deveined
¾ cup tomatoes, chopped
1 pinch saffron
1 Tbsp. salt
½ tsp. yellow food color
2 cups seafood broth OR water
1 cup Valencia rice
green peas, pimiento, parsley for garnish

In heavy frying pan, heat olive oil and sauté chopped garlic, onion and green pepper about 3 minutes. Add raw shrimp and as soon as they turn pink, add tomatoes, saffron, salt, color and seafood broth. Bring to a boil and add rice. Stir well; transfer to casserole and bake covered in 350°F oven about 1 hour, or until rice is tender. Serve hot, topped with cooked green peas, pimiento and parsley. **Serves 2.**

Shrimp Waikiki

1 pound raw shrimp
1 9-oz. can sliced pineapple
½ cup brown sugar
½ cup vinegar
2 Tbsp. soy sauce
1¼ cups water
3 Tbsp. cornstarch
1 green pepper, cut in strips
1 tomato, cut in wedges
hot cooked rice

Cook shrimp in boiling water 3 to 4 minutes (see page 101). Drain syrup from pineapple into saucepan. Cut pineapple slices in half and set aside. Add brown sugar, vinegar, soy sauce and 1 cup water to pineapple syrup. Bring to boil. Combine cornstarch with ¼ cup cold water. Add to syrup mixture and cook, stirring constantly, until thickened. Stir in green pepper, pineapple, tomato wedges. Cook over medium heat 2 minutes. Add shrimp and cook just until heated through. Serve hot, in a circle of hot white rice. **Serves 4.**

Party Time Shrimp Dip

1½ pounds cooked, peeled, deveined shrimp, fresh or frozen
1 16-oz. container whipped cream cheese
1 cup mayonnaise
1 Tbsp. Worcestershire sauce
2 tsp. liquid hot pepper sauce
2 Tbsp. green onion tops, chopped

Thaw shrimp if frozen. Coarsely chop shrimp. In small bowl, combine all ingredients. Refrigerate several hours or overnight. Serve with crisp crackers or corn chips. **Makes 3 cups of dip.**

Shrimp Foo Yung

- 5 beaten eggs
- 1 cup cooked fresh or canned shrimp
- ¼ cup thinly sliced water chestnuts
- ½ cup mushrooms, thinly sliced
- 1 cup onion, finely chopped
- 3 Tbsp. soy sauce
- 2 Tbsp. butter or margarine
- 1 Tbsp. cornstarch
- ¼ cup bouillon (made from cubes)
- ¼ tsp. sugar

Stir shrimp, water chestnuts, mushrooms and onions into eggs, and mix until well blended. Add 2 tablespoons soy sauce; stir to blend. Place butter or margarine in skillet over low heat. Pour in egg mixture and cook until lightly browned on one side. Turn to brown on other side.

Meanwhile, combine 1 tablespoon soy sauce, cornstarch, bouillon and sugar in small saucepan. Simmer over low heat. Turn Shrimp Foo Yung out onto warmed plate; cover with sauce. **Serves 4.**

Chinese Stir-Fry Shrimp with Vegetables

- 1 Tbsp. cornstarch
- 3 Tbsp. water
- ½ cup chicken broth or water
- 1 Tbsp. soy sauce
- dash sugar
- 6–8oz. raw shrimp, shelled, deveined and halved horizontally, if large
- 1½ tsp. minced fresh ginger root, divided
- 1 clove garlic, minced
- 2 Tbsp. oil, divided
- 4 oz. snow peas, stems and strings removed
- 1 cup bok choy or celery, sliced
- ¼ cup green onion, sliced diagonally
- 1 cup Chinese cabbage or cabbage, coarsely shredded
- hot cooked rice

Combine cornstarch and water. Stir in chicken broth, soy sauce and sugar. Set aside. Stir fry shrimp, ½ teaspoon ginger and garlic in 1 tablespoon oil in a large skillet or wok over medium high heat, cooking 2 to 3 minutes or just until pink.

Drain shrimp on paper towels and set aside. Heat remaining tablespoon oil in same skillet. Add snow peas, bok choy, green onion, and remaining teaspoon ginger. Stir fry 2 minutes. Add Chinese cabbage and stir fry 1 to 2 minutes or until vegetables are tender crisp. Add cornstarch mixture and reserved shrimp. Cook and stir 1 to 2 minutes, or until sauce is slightly thickened. Serve over rice. **Serves 2.**

Shrimp Fried Rice

¼ cup butter, margarine or oil
2 cups cooked shrimp, halved
2 tsp. salt
½ tsp. pepper
2 eggs, beaten lightly
5 cups cooked rice
3 Tbsp. soy sauce
3 green onions, chopped
¼ cup canned mushroom slices
¼ cup green pepper, diced
¼ cup water chestnuts, sliced
1 cup bean sprouts, drained

Heat 1 tablespoon oil in skillet or wok over medium high heat. Stir fry onions, mushrooms, green pepper, water chestnuts and bean sprouts 1 to 2 minutes or just until tender crisp. Set aside.

Reduce heat to medium. Pour remaining oil or butter into skillet. Add shrimp, salt and pepper; cook 2 to 3 minutes until lightly browned. Stir in eggs, blending well. Add rice and cook until golden in color. Stir in prepared vegetables; cook just until entire mixture is hot. Serve on heated plates. **Serves 6.**

Spanish Shrimp-Olive Omelet

4 eggs, separated
2 Tbsp. milk
dash cayenne pepper
⅛ tsp. pepper
1 5-oz. can shrimp, drained, OR 1 cup cooked shrimp
1 Tbsp. chives, snipped
⅓ cup pimiento-stuffed olives, chopped
¼ cup melted butter or margarine
½ cup green pepper, chopped
1 16-oz. can tomatoes
1 tsp. onion salt

Preheat oven to 350°F. Beat egg whites until stiff but not dry. Combine egg yolks, milk, cayenne and pepper. Beat until foamy. Fold egg whites, shrimp, olives and chives into egg yolk mixture.

Heat 2 tablespoons butter in skillet and add egg mixture. Cook over medium heat until bottom browns. Place skillet in oven 15 minutes or until eggs are firm.

Meanwhile, combine remaining 2 tablespoons butter and green pepper. Sauté until tender. Add tomatoes and onion salt. Cover and cook 15 minutes. Remove omelet from oven and turn onto heated plate; top with half of tomato mixture. Fold omelet and pour remaining tomato mixture on top. Serve hot. **Serves 4.**

Beer-Battered Fried Shrimp

¼ cup beer
½ cup water
1 Tbsp. vegetable oil
1 cup sifted flour
¼ tsp. salt
1 egg white, beaten stiff
2 pounds raw shrimp

To make batter, combine beer, water and oil. Sift in flour and salt. Stir only until blended. Fold in stiff egg white. If necessary, add a bit more water to make a thin batter.

Peel and devein shrimp, leaving on tails. Dip shrimp in batter. Heat skillet with deep hot fat to 375°F and fry shrimp 2 to 3 minutes, just until pink. Serve hot with French fries and cole slaw. (Note: This recipe is also good with shelled, chopped lobster tails substituted for the shrimp; increase frying time to 4 – 5 minutes.) **Serves 4.**

Arroz Con Camarones

(Beer-simmered shrimp with rice)

2 pounds raw shrimp, shelled
4 cups beer
2 Tbsp. lemon juice
1 tsp. salt
¼ tsp. freshly ground black pepper
1 bay leaf
3 Tbsp. butter
½ cup onion, chopped fine
1 cup uncooked rice
¾ cup green pepper, diced
½ pound fresh mushrooms, sliced
1 8-oz. jar pimientos, sliced

Wash and devein shrimp under cold running water. In large pan, combine shrimp, beer, lemon juice, salt, pepper and bay leaf. Bring to a boil; reduce heat to simmer and cook 5 minutes. Drain, saving the stock. Refrigerate shrimp.

In a saucepan, melt butter and stir in onion and rice; cook over medium heat until lightly browned, stirring mixture constantly. Add shrimp stock, green pepper and mushrooms. Cover; reduce heat to low and simmer 15 minutes or until rice is tender. (Check instructions on rice box for exact cooking time.) Just before serving, stir in shrimp and pimientos. Add salt and pepper to taste, if needed, and serve hot. (For tropical Florida taste, serve with a crisp green salad topped with guacamole dressing.) **Serves 4 to 6.**

Italian Scampi

2 lb. uncooked jumbo shrimp
4 Tbsp. fine, dry bread crumbs
½ cup butter, melted
½ cup olive oil
4 cloves garlic, crushed
salt, pepper to taste
dash cayenne pepper
¼ cup finely chopped parsley

Do not shell shrimp; split them in half almost through, leaving tail unsplit. Flatten and place shrimp, shell down, in shallow broiler pan. Sprinkle lightly with bread crumbs. Mix together melted butter, crushed garlic and olive oil. Drizzle sauce over shrimp and broil 4 to 5 inches below heat for about 5 minutes, or until shrimp turn pink. Use tongs to place shrimp in heated deep dish. Pour garlic sauce over shrimp; sprinkle with cayenne, salt, pepper and parsley. Serve hot, with plenty of lemon wedges. **Serves 4.**

Broiled Rock Shrimp

2½ pounds split, deveined rock shrimp, fresh or frozen
½ cup margarine or butter, melted
¾ tsp. salt
¼ tsp. white pepper
¼ tsp. paprika
Lemon Butter Sauce (recipe below)

Thaw rock shrimp if frozen. If not purchased split, place rock shrimp on cutting board with swimmerettes (legs) exposed. With sharp knife, make a cut between the swimmerettes through the meat to the hard shell. Spread the shell open until it is flat, butterfly style, and wash thoroughly in cold water to remove sand vein. Lay rock shrimp flat on greased broiling pan with meat exposed. Baste with margarine. Sprinkle with salt, white pepper and paprika. Broil 4 inches below heat about 2 minutes or until meat is opaque. Serve hot with Lemon Butter Sauce. **Serves 6.**

Lemon Butter Sauce

½ cup margarine or butter, melted
2 Tbsp. lemon juice or lime juice

Combine margarine and lemon juice. Heat. **Makes about ½ cup sauce.**

Coconut Fried Shrimp with Mango Sauce

(A specialty of Reflections on the Bay at Miamarina)

2 pounds raw shrimp
1 cup all-purpose flour
½ tsp. sugar
½ tsp. salt
1 egg, slightly beaten
2 Tbsp. vegetable oil
⅔ cup grated coconut
Mango Sauce (recipe below)

Thaw shrimp, if they are frozen; shell and devein, leaving tails intact. Blot shrimp dry with paper towels. In large bowl, combine flour, sugar, salt, egg, oil. Dip shrimp into batter and then into coconut. Fry in deep fat fryer at 375°F until golden brown. Serve with Mango Sauce. **Serves 4 to 6.**

Mango Sauce

2 mangoes, peeled, seeded and chopped
4 shallots, thinly sliced
4 cloves garlic, thinly sliced
½ oz. fresh gingerroot
1 oz. tamarind paste
2 inches sliced lemon peel
2 inches sliced orange peel
1 cup light brown sugar, firmly packed
2 cups cider vinegar
1 tsp. cayenne pepper
⅓ tsp. cinnamon
⅓ tsp. ground cardamom
1 Tbsp. Kosher salt
8 bananas

In heavy, stainless steel saucepan (*not* aluminum), place vinegar and sugar; bring to a boil. Reduce heat and simmer until thick syrup forms and thickens (238°F on candy thermometer). Add all other ingredients except bananas; simmer 45 minutes, stirring frequently. Remove from heat and chill. In blender or food processor, puree mango mixture and bananas until smooth and well blended. Store covered in a glass container in refrigerator until needed. Serve cold with hot, freshly cooked coconut shrimp. Dip and enjoy!

Oriental Shrimp Salad

(Makes 12 ounces of shrimp serve four hungry adults.)

¾ lb. cooked, peeled, deveined shrimp, fresh or frozen
1 10-oz. package frozen peas, cooked and drained
1 cup celery, finely chopped
½ cup mayonnaise
1 Tbsp. lemon or lime juice
½ tsp. curry powder
⅛ tsp. garlic salt
⅛ tsp. white pepper
1 3-oz. can chow mein noodles
½ cup salted cashew nuts
salad greens

Thaw shrimp if frozen. Cut large shrimp in half. Combine first 8 ingredients in large bowl; mix well and chill. Add noodles and nuts and toss lightly. Serve on your favorite salad greens. **Serves 4.**

Shrimp Creole

- 1/4 cup salt pork, chopped fine
- 1/2 cup celery, chopped fine
- 1 large onion, chopped fine
- 1 Tbsp. sugar
- 1 28-oz. can tomatoes, chopped
- 3/4 cup chili sauce
- 1/3 cup tomato paste
- 1 clove garlic, minced
- 1 Tbsp. beef-flavored gravy base
- 1/2 tsp. dried thyme, crushed
- 3/4 tsp. salt, (or more, to taste)
- 1/4 tsp. pepper
- 1 1/2 pounds shrimp, cooked and shelled
- hot cooked rice

In large frying pan, fry salt pork until crisp; remove pork bits. In the drippings, sauté celery and onion until softened, but not brown. Add sugar, tomatoes, chili sauce, tomato paste, garlic, gravy base, thyme, salt and pepper. Cover and simmer 30 minutes. Stir in shrimp; heat just until shrimp are hot. Serve at once over hot cooked rice. (Note: Garlic bread goes great with this!) **Serves 6 to 8.**

Shrimp Ratatouille

- 1 pound raw, peeled, deveined shrimp, fresh or frozen
- 1/4 cup olive or salad oil
- 2 small zucchini squash, unpeeled and thinly sliced
- 1 small eggplant, peeled and cut in 1-inch cubes
- 1 medium onion, thinly sliced
- 1 cup sliced mushrooms
- 1 medium green pepper, seeded, cut in 1-inch pieces
- 1 16-oz. can tomato wedges
- 1 1/2 tsp. garlic salt
- 1 tsp. crushed basil
- 1 tsp. dried parsley
- 1/4 tsp. pepper

Thaw shrimp if frozen. Cut in half lengthwise. In large frying pan, sauté zucchini, eggplant, onion, mushrooms and green pepper in oil 10 minutes or until tender crisp. Add shrimp and cook 2 minutes, stirring frequently. Add tomatoes, garlic salt, basil, parsley and pepper. Cover; simmer about 5 minutes or until shrimp are tender. Serve with rice or noodles. **Serves 6.**

"Can-venient" Cooking from the Pantry

Although here in Florida we're blessed with an abundance of fresh seafood year round, for the sake of convenience it's nice to keep a few cans of seafood in the cupboard. Cans of tuna, salmon, crab, clams and sardines can be found in most supermarkets, and they're great for whipping together an impromptu meal.

Clam Chowder Pie

¾ cup cornmeal
1½ cups sifted all-purpose flour
1 tsp. salt
⅔ cup lard
½ cup milk
2 cans condensed clam chowder
1 7-oz. can minced clams, drained
2 cups cooked canned potatoes, halved
½ tsp. white wine Worcestershire

Sift together cornmeal, flour and salt. Cut in lard until mixture resembles coarse crumbs. Add milk all at once, mixing with fork until dough forms a ball. Divide pastry into 6 parts. On lightly floured board, roll each part to form a circle about ⅛ inch thick. Fit circles into individual oven-proof casseroles (1½ cup size); flute edges of dough.

Combine clam chowder, minced clams, potatoes and Worcestershire sauce. Place mixture in pastry-lined casseroles. Bake in preheated 375°F oven 25 to 30 minutes until crust is lightly browned and filling hot and bubbly. Try this with buttered green peas and a chilly tomato-olive aspic. **Serves 6.**

Clams in Aspic

1 envelope unflavored gelatin
½ cup cold water
1 16-oz. jar piccalilli (regular or hot)
2 7½-oz. cans minced clams, drained
1 lemon or lime, sliced
mayonnaise

Soak gelatin in cold water 5 minutes. Combine piccalilli and minced clams. Heat in saucepan to a simmer. Add softened gelatin and stir until dissolved. Remove from heat; pour into individual molds (or a single large one), rinsed with cold water. Chill until firm, and serve on crisp lettuce with lemon slices and mayonnaise. **Serves 4 to 6.**

Busy Mom's Creamed Tuna

½ cup celery, sliced
2 Tbsp. onion, chopped
1 Tbsp. butter or margarine
1 11-oz. can condensed Cheddar cheese soup
½ cup milk
1 7-oz. can tuna, drained, flaked
2 Tbsp. pimiento, chopped
chopped parsley
hot cooked rice or toast triangles

In saucepan, cook celery and onion in butter until tender. Blend in soup and milk. Add tuna and pimiento. Heat, stirring occasionally. Serve over hot rice or toast triangles, sprinkled with chopped parsley. Try this with Harvard beets and a salad of tomatoes marinated in vinaigrette dressing. **Serves 4.**

Macaroni Tuna-Olive Salad

2 cups (8 oz.) elbow macaroni
½ cup sliced stuffed olives
¼ cup onion, chopped
1 7-oz. can solid pack tuna, drained
2 Tbsp. lemon or lime juice
¼ tsp. celery salt
½ tsp. salt
⅔ cup mayonnaise

Cook macaroni in rapidly boiling salted water, as instructed on package. Stir now and then. Drain in colander; rinse with cold water and allow to drain thoroughly. Combine macaroni with olives, onion, tuna, lime or lemon juice, celery salt, salt and mayonnaise. Chill well and keep refrigerated until ready to serve. (Note: Some folks like to add a spoonful of celery seed and sliced celery to this recipe.) **Serves 4.**

Shrimp Salad Rolls

1 4½-oz. can shrimp
2 hard-cooked eggs
2 tsp. green onion, chopped
¼ cup mayonnaise
2 tsp. mustard with horseradish
dash freshly ground pepper
2 to 3 big bakery rolls

Drain and chop shrimp; chop eggs finely. Mix with onion, mayonnaise, mustard and pepper. Cut a slice from the top of the rolls. Scoop out center of bottom half. Spread inside lightly with mayonnaise. Fill rolls with shrimp salad and replace tops. You might like this with an avocado and grapefruit salad, moistened with tart French dressing. **Serves 2 to 3.**

Four-Star Deviled Seafood
(for a Crowd)

6 Florida grapefruit
5 Tbsp. butter or margarine
6 Tbsp. flour
1 tsp. salt
1½ cups milk
1 tsp. dry mustard
½ tsp. Tabasco sauce
1 16-oz. can pink salmon
1 7-oz. can white tuna
1 7½-oz. can crabmeat
½ pound fresh cooked shrimp, shelled
1½ cups coarsely crushed potato chips

Clean grapefruit and cut in half. Cut around each section, loosening fruit from membrane. Remove segments. Reserve 3 cups of the segments to use with seafood. Cut out membrane and scrape fruit halves with a spoon to clean thoroughly.

Melt butter, then add flour, salt and mustard; stir to a smooth paste. Add milk and cook, stirring constantly until mixture thickens and comes to a boil. Remove from heat; stir in Tabasco.

Drain and flake tuna and salmon; drain and shred crabmeat, removing any bits of shell. Cook and devein shrimp, and cut into bite-size pieces. Stir all seafood into sauce. Add drained grapefruit segments and mix lightly.

Fill grapefruit shells with seafood mixture; sprinkle top with crushed potato chips. Bake in 350°F oven for 45 minutes.

Garnish with radish roses. Serve with warm bubble bread, inviting guests to pull a chunk from a large loaf, and if you like, a crisp cabbage-and-pineapple cole slaw. Super! **Serves 12.**

Sardine Spread (or Dip)

1 8-oz. package cream cheese
2 cans sardines
2 Tbsp. onion, finely chopped
1 tsp. parsley, chopped
¼ tsp. salt (optional)
½ tsp. white wine Worcestershire
1 tsp. lime or lemon juice
cream (if making dip)

Soften cream cheese at room temperature. Mash sardines in their oil. Combine cheese, sardines, onion, parsley, salt (if used), Worcestershire and lime juice. Blend well. Use as spread for crackers or melba toast. To convert to a dip, thin the mixture with cream. **Makes about 2 cups.**

Curried Salmon Tahiti in Coconut Shells

(Once you get the coconuts open, this recipe is easy — and delicious!)

4 medium coconuts
4 tablespoons butter or margarine
½ medium onion, minced
2 cloves garlic, minced
¼ tsp. pepper
¼ tsp. hot pepper flakes
2 tsp. curry powder
6 Tbsp. flour
1 16-oz. can salmon
2½ cups coconut water or milk
4 Tbsp. mango chutney, chopped, including syrup
½ tsp. salt
juice of half a lime
½ cup diced canned papaya

Saw tops off coconuts or strike glancing blows with a hammer around the coconut on the opposite end from the eyes, until the shell cracks and the top may be removed. Leave coconut meat in the large part of the shell, but remove it from the tops; shred it and toast in oven.

In saucepan, melt butter. Add onion and garlic; sauté 10 minutes or until onion is soft. Add pepper, hot pepper flakes (increase hot pepper to ½ teaspoon for very hot curry) and curry powder — either mild, medium or hot, as you choose. Cook 5 minutes longer. Stir in flour. Add liquid from can of salmon and gradually stir in coconut water or milk. Cook, stirring until sauce is thick and smooth. Flake salmon and stir into sauce, along with chutney, salt, lime juice and papaya.

Spoon mixture into coconut shells. Fasten tops in place with a paste of flour and water. Arrange in shallow baking dish, and pour in warm water to a depth of one inch. Bake in 350°F oven for 1 hour.

Serve in coconut shells with cooked rice, and pass dishes of chutney, toasted coconut, chopped peanuts and chopped preserved ginger, which guests may pile up on top of the curry. **Serves 4.**

Monterey Souffle Salad

1 pkg. lemon gelatin
1 cup hot water
½ cup cold water
2 Tbsp. lemon or lime juice
½ cup mayonnaise
¼ tsp. salt
¾ cup cucumber, chopped
1½ cups chunk-style tuna, drained
¼ cup pimiento-stuffed olives, sliced
2 Tbsp. pimiento, chopped
½ tsp. onion, grated
salad greens

Dissolve gelatin in hot water. With rotary beater, blend in cold water, lemon juice, mayonnaise and salt. Pour into refrigerator freezing tray. Quick chill in freezing unit 15 to 20 minutes until firm about 1 inch from the edges.

Whip mixture with beater until fluffy. Fold in tuna, cucumber, olives, pimiento and onion. Turn into a lightly oiled 1-quart mold. Chill until firm in refrigerator (not freezing unit) 1 hour or until set. Unmold onto a bed of crisp salad greens. Great with hot little muffins — apple, pecan or carrot. **Serves 4 to 6.**

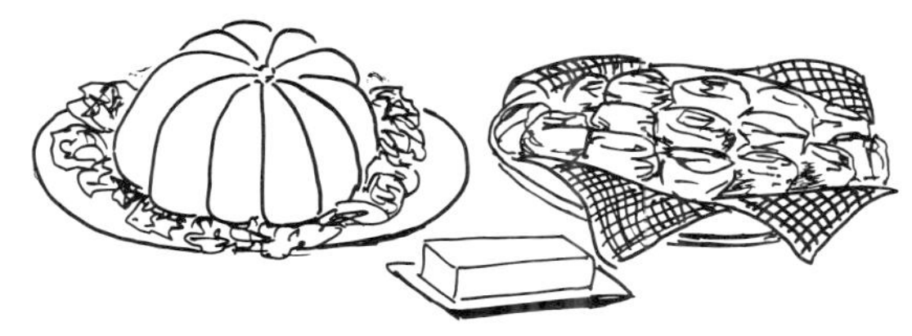

Outdoor Cooking - Florida Style

If you limit yourself to chicken, pork or beef when you get out the barbecue grill, it's time to extend your cookout talents to include fish and seafood!

Why? Because these treats from the deep cook quickly, taste delicious. Fish is more tender than red meat, because it has no connective tissue. Florida has a great variety to choose from — and it's soooo good for you, so low in cholesterol compared to most meat, yet rich in protein and healthful polyunsaturated Omega-3 oils. (For more about this, read the chapter on Nutritional Fish Facts.)

Florida has hundreds of parks and beaches that beg to be visited, or you can set up the grill in your yard, out by the pool or aboard a boat. To cap off an active day of swimming, boating or fishing, there's nothing more fun than a picnic in the sunshine or dinner under our magnificent Florida moon.

Picture yourself sitting beside a crackling campfire along a tropical river, listening to birdsong and sniffing the smoky smell of burning hickory chips blending with the great aroma of a big pot of spicy catfish stew — preferably filled with your own freshly caught catfish. You grab a big bowl of stew, slather sweet butter on a slice of cornbread from an old-fashioned skillet, and sip a mug of good hot coffee. That's out-of-this-world good eating, Florida style!

Or maybe you prefer garlicky shrimp kebobs broiled over hot coals. Or fish fried to crisp goodness in a heavy iron skillet, surrounded with crunchy little hushpuppies. You have no end of delicious dishes awaiting you!

Cooking Equipment

You can make the cookout scene with any equipment you choose, from simple to superlative. My favorite is an old standby — a smoke-cooker grill with a dome cover that serves double duty as a straight grill or smoke cooker. The speed and convenience of cooking on the gas-fired grill make it a great favorite. You might like a slow-cooking water smoker (charcoal, gas or electric), a simple, inexpensive free-standing grill or even a small hibachi. Easiest of all (especially at the beach) is a hole dug in the sand, with rocks at bottom and around it, and a wire grill placed on top. Fire up the coals and you're ready to cook.

A word to the wise. Most barbecue units are sold with an instruction sheet or cookbook. You will save yourself time and (frequently) wasted effort if you take the time to read the instructions before you start cooking. You would be surprised how many people run into trouble because they rush into cooking without learning how the unit operates.

Tips for the Outdoor Chef

It's important that you buy the freshest, best quality seafood you can afford, and give it the sniff test before you buy. Keep it wrapped in plastic wrap and on ice until cooking time. It can deteriorate quickly in Florida's warm climate. Do have your grill clean and well-oiled each time you use it, because fish has a tendency to stick.

You can keep your fish in one piece, and turn it more easily, if you use a hinged wire basket. You place the well-oiled fish inside, cook on one side, turn the basket and cook the other side. So easy! Brush with more oil or marinade while it is cooking. A three-pound fish should take 25 to 35 minutes.

Wood or Charcoal?

Now about fuel. Some serious outdoor chefs find it difficult to regulate heat for precise cooking times using a bed of coals. For them, wood is the only way to go. Hickory, oak and mesquite are favorites, plus many more. You may use pine, but be aware that it burns quickly and produces a great deal of smoke.

Charcoal has long been the favorite barbecue fuel in the U.S. and has grown even more popular since the new light-and-burn packages have made it much easier to get the fire going in a hurry. You can of course, use a liquid charcoal fluid to help things along.

These tips may help you when you grill with charcoal:

1. Stack regular charcoal in a pyramid-shaped pile, and douse it with starter fluid.

2. Always start the fire 30 to 45 minutes before you plan to start cooking, so that it has time to burn down to gray, hot coals.

3. Reduce or increase heat by raising or lowering the grill. Bringing grill and charcoal closer together will produce a hotter fire. It's best to leave a corner where there are very few coals, where cooked food can be kept warm while the rest of the dinner is cooking.

4. Cook fish about 5 inches above the coals, following the rule of allowing 10 minutes of cooking time for each inch thickness of the fish.

5. Keep a water bottle with sprinkler top handy (a soda bottle works fine), to douse any flames that flare up — unless you like a charred taste, and most folks don't.

You may ask, is it possible to cook over charcoal and get a pronounced flavor of wood smoke? Yes, indeed. Add liquid smoke to the marinade or basting sauce used with fish or seafood. Or toss a few chips of aromatic wood, such as oak, hickory, lemon or orange wood on the fire, just before the food is removed from the grill.

Marinades add zesty flavor, but when you place food in marinade before grilling, watch your timing! The leaner the fish, the shorter time it should be marinated. Too much time in a marinade can cause fish fibers to break down. It is possible to grill fatty fish such as mackerel without using a marinade — perhaps just brush it with butter while it cooks. But even with fatty fish, a really good marinade is the way to add succulent flavor.

(For a list of fat and lean fish, see the chapter on Nutritional Fish Facts.)

Don't Forget the Foil

A griller's best friend is aluminum foil — great for steaming or poaching, especially rather fragile, tender fish less than one inch thick. Foil catches drippings, protects from the wind, and lets you cook without soiling pots and pans. Also, it's easy to pack and carry. Again, to prevent sticking, grease the inside of the foil before wrapping it around the food.

Use foil, too, for whole fish or fish steaks, covered if you like with vegetables and lemon slices. You know how a fish tail can burn before the rest of the fish is cooked? The answer is to wrap the tail in foil before grilling. Shellfish also cooks beautifully in foil. Just place seafood and sauce or other ingredients inside the foil (greased of course), fold and seal by pressing edges together tightly.

As everyone knows, the most delicious go-alongs such as corn on the cob or baking potatoes can be wrapped in foil and cooked over the coals. A medium-sized potato cooks in 45 to 60 minutes; corn on the cob, spread with butter and wrapped in foil, cooks in about 25 minutes and should be turned two or three times. If the fire is very hot and corn is to be placed on the coals, double the foil and twist the ends to secure.

Buying Fish for the Grill

You may grill whole fish or pieces cut to serving size. If fish goes directly onto the grill, it's best to use thick steaks, fillets and fish 8 to 10 inches long. Here are explanations of some terms you will encounter at the market:

Fillets — Boneless sides of fish cut lengthwise from the backbone.

Steaks — Large dressed fish yielding cross-section slices, including a section of backbone.

Whole or Round — Fish as it was caught. It must be cleaned and scaled, with head, tail and fins removed.

Dressed — Fish which has been scaled and cleaned (usually with head, tail and fins removed). It's ready for the grill.

Serving Size — Figure a third to a half pound of fillets per serving (depending on appetites), the same for steaks. But with whole or dressed fish, you will need about one pound per person.

Ready? Get Set... Let's Barbecue!

How long should fish cook on the grill? The condition of the coals, the amount of wind and thickness of fish all influence the length of cooking time. Measure raw fish at the thickest place after stuffing or rolling, then allow 10 minutes cooking time per inch. Your coals should be medium hot, with fish in a wire basket or on the grill and about five inches from the heat.

Grilling ice-cold fish will take a bit longer. The same is true if fish is wrapped in foil, so figure another 5 minutes of cooking time per inch.

When the fish is very large, move the grill farther from the coals — about eight inches — so the fish won't burn on the outside before it cooks on the inside.

To test for doneness, cut a tiny slice to the backbone. There should be no pinkness and the meat should be opaque, not translucent (as our recipes so often state), it should flake easily when tested with a fork. Above all, *do not overcook fish or seafood!*

You may cook a whole fish right on the coals this way: Grease a large piece of foil; wrap the fish in several pieces of bacon, wrap and seal it in the foil. (You may add slices of onion and lemon, if you like.) Place the bundle right on top of the hot, gray coals and cook about 20 minutes. Fillets will cook the same way, needing only 10 to 15 minutes.

To make super barbecued shrimp, marinate the shrimp in your favorite marinade, drain and place in a greased wire basket or slide onto skewers. With the shrimp about five inches above the hot coals, allow one to two minutes per side, basting at least once with butter or marinade.

Whatever your preference, you have an excellent variety of fish and seafood from tropical waters to cook on your grill. You are sure to delight friends and family with the marvelous taste and, as a bonus, supply health-giving nutrition with these high-protein, low-calorie fish treats.

So, delay no longer. Get outdoors. Fire up the grill and enjoy!

Blackened Catfish Fillets, Creole Style

1 Tbsp. paprika
½ tsp. salt
1 tsp. onion powder
1 tsp. garlic powder
1 tsp. cayenne pepper
¾ tsp. white pepper
¾ tsp. black pepper
½ tsp. thyme
½ tsp. oregano
4 farm-raised catfish fillets
½ cup melted butter
lemon wedges

Combine first 9 ingredients in small bowl. Start barbecue fire and allow to burn down to gray coals. Place heavy skillet on grill over coals. Dip fillets in melted butter, then in seasoning mixture. When skillet is very hot, place seasoned fillets in pan and cook 2 to 3 minutes per side until blackened. Serve with a squeeze of fresh lemon. **Serves 4.**

Deep-Fried Catfish

6 pounds catfish steaks
1 tsp. salt (or more, to taste)
¼ tsp. pepper
1 1-pound package cornbread mix
1 cup white all-purpose flour
1 tsp. lemon pepper
1 tsp. paprika
1 quart vegetable oil

If fish is freshly caught, clean and skin; cut into steaks. If frozen, thaw before cooking (preferably in the refrigerator). Season steaks with salt and pepper; wrap loosely in waxed paper and refrigerate at least one hour. Light fire and allow to burn down to gray coals. In plastic bag, shake together cornmeal mixture, flour, lemon pepper and paprika. Fill a heavy iron skillet with deep sides with at least 3 inches of oil and heat over fire until very hot. Keep a small stock of wood pieces nearby, to feed the fire and keep it very hot while you cook. Place fish in hot oil, turning once with spatula and figuring about 10 minutes total cooking time for each inch of fish thickness. If desired, serve on thick slices of toasted French bread. **Serves 6 to 8.**

Cook's Tip: *You may want to mix your chosen fish coating — such as cornmeal and seasonings — in a plastic bag in your kitchen, ahead of time. Then, carry the prepared mixture to the barbecue, ready to use. A handy time-saver!*

Outdoor Fish Fry

(Take your pick of bluefish, snapper, freshwater bass or grouper.)

¼ cup evaporated milk
1½ tsp. salt
dash pepper
½ cup all-purpose flour
¼ cup cornmeal
1 tsp. paprika
2 pounds fish fillets, or small fish, cleaned and split
¼ cup melted fat or vegetable oil

Combine milk, salt and pepper. In separate dish, mix flour, cornmeal and paprika. Dip fish in milk mixture; roll in flour mixture. Place deep, heavy iron skillet about 4 inches above hot coals, pour in fat or oil and heat until hot but not smoking. Slip coated fish into hot oil and fry about 4 minutes; turn and fry other side 3 to 4 minutes, until done and nicely browned. Drain on absorbent paper. (Great with corn on the cob baked in foil atop the coals.) **Serves 5.**

Cook's Tip: *When frying fish outdoors, you will get good results by covering the bottom of a heavy frying pan with ¼ inch of vegetable oil, peanut oil, melted shortening or whatever oil you choose.*

Barbecued Rock Lobster with Brown Butter Sauce

6 4-oz. rock lobster tails
½ cup butter or margarine
4 Tbsp. tarragon vinegar
1 tsp. Worcestershire sauce
2 Tbsp. chopped parsley
lemon or lime wedges

Thaw frozen lobster tails in refrigerator. With kitchen shears, cut along each edge of thin underside membrane and remove. Grasp tails in both hands and bend backwards toward shell side very sharply to crack in about 3 places. Or insert long skewers between meat and shell, to prevent curling.

Meanwhile, melt butter in skillet and brown it, watching carefully so it does not burn. Add vinegar, Worcestershire sauce and parsley. Mix well. Keep warm on grill while cooking lobster tails.

Grease shells of rock lobster tails and place on grill over glowing gray coals, shell side down. Grill for 5 minutes on shell side. Baste flesh side liberally with brown butter sauce. Turn meat side down and grill 5 minutes longer. Lobster is done when the flesh is opaque and creamy white. Serve at once with remaining brown butter sauce, garnished with lemon or lime wedges. **Serves 6.**

Lobster Tails Grilled in Foil

6 spiny lobster tails, fresh or frozen
¼ cup butter or margarine, melted
2 Tbsp. lemon or lime juice
½ tsp. salt
pepper, freshly ground
melted butter for dipping

Thaw lobster tails in refrigerator if frozen. Start fire in grill 30 minutes before cooking time. If lobster is fresh, remove swimmerettes and sharp edges. Cut 6 squares of heavy-duty aluminum foil, 12 inches each. Place each lobster tail on half of each square of foil. Combine ¼ cup butter, lemon or lime juice, salt and pepper. Baste lobster meat with sauce. Fold other half of foil over lobster tail; seal edges by making double folds in foil. Place packages of lobster tails on barbecue grill, shell side down, 5 inches above hot coals. Cook 20 minutes. Remove lobster tails from foil. On well-greased grill, place lobster tails, meaty side down, for 2 to 3 minutes, or until nicely browned. Serve at once with melted butter. (This is equally good with 2 or 3 pounds of fresh shrimp substituted for the lobster. Place the shelled shrimp on skewers before wrapping in foil, for easy removal and browning over the coals. You may also eliminate the lemon butter and instead combine white wine, soy sauce and ground ginger with the black pepper for the marinade, for shrimp, oriental style.) **Serves 6.**

Barbecued Snapper Fillets

1 cup catsup
½ cup frozen lemonade concentrate, thawed and undiluted
2 green onions, finely chopped
1 clove garlic, minced
4 bay leaves
⅛ tsp. salt
⅛ tsp. pepper
1 tsp. prepared mustard
4 1-pound red snapper fillets
vegetable oil

To make marinade, place first 8 ingredients in large shallow glass dish; stir well. Place fillets in marinade, turning to coat well; cover and refrigerate one hour. Meanwhile, start fire and let it burn down to coals.

Drain fillets and save the marinade. Place fillets in well-oiled wire basket with long handle and grill about 5 inches above hot coals 5 to 7 minutes on each side or until fish flakes easily. Brush with marinade while cooking. Remove bay leaves and serve fish with heated marinade, which guests may use as sauce. Serve with red ripe tomato slices topped with guacamole, and toasted French bread. **Serves 4.**

Eel Over the Coals

- 2 pounds eel, skinned, cut in 2-inch pieces
- ½ cup milk
- 2 Tbsp. parsley, finely chopped
- 2 cups crumbs from day-old French bread
- 2 Tbsp. salt
- olive oil or vegetable oil

Start fire and allow it to burn down to coals. Mix together bread crumbs from day-old French bread with chopped parsley. Dip eel pieces into milk, then into the crumb mixture. Place on oiled aluminum foil and refrigerate 15 minutes. Slip onto skewers and cook on well-oiled grill (4 to 6 inches above the coals) for about 15 minutes, brushing with oil as needed. After 10 minutes, remove eel pieces from the heat and sprinkle with salt, then return to grill for remaining 5 minutes of cooking time. Serve with spicy brown mustard and crisp tomato and cucumber salad. **Serves 4.**

Grilled Oriental Swordfish

- 4 swordfish steaks, ¾-inch thick
- ¼ cup Kikkoman Lite soy sauce
- 3 Tbsp. minced onion
- 1 Tbsp. fresh ginger root, chopped
- 1 Tbsp. sesame seed, toasted
- ½ tsp. sugar

Place fish in single layer in shallow glass baking pan. Measure soy sauce, onion, ginger, sesame seed and sugar into blender container; process on low speed 30 seconds, scraping sides down once. Pour sauce over fish, turning to coat both sides. Marinate 30 minutes in refrigerator, turning fish occasionally. Remove fish and grill 4 inches from heat source of moderately hot coals 5 minutes on each side, or until fish flakes easily. Brush once with marinade while cooking. Serve hot. **Serves 4.**

Grilled Scallop Kebobs

- 1½ pounds shelled scallops
- 1 tsp. salt
- ½ pound bacon, cut into 1½-inch pieces
- ¼ pound (1 stick) butter, melted
- hot buttered toast
- tartar sauce
- chopped parsley

Soak scallops in cold water in refrigerator for one hour. Have ready a large saucepan filled with boiling water salted with one teaspoon or more of salt. Drop scallops into hot water for 2 minutes. Remove; drain, patting dry with paper towels. Start fire; wait until coals are gray with no flames. On skewers, alternate scallops with bacon pieces. Cook over hot coals until bacon is crisp.

Baste with melted butter as needed. Slip scallops off skewers onto hot buttered toast; sprinkle with chopped parsley and add a big dollop of tartar sauce. **Serves 4 to 6.**

Angels on Horseback

2 dozen oysters
juice of 2 lemons
2 Tbsp. paprika
12 slices bacon, cut in half
6 slices buttered toast, cut in half
lemon slices
watercress

Start fire and reduce to hot gray coals. Pat oysters dry with paper towels; season lightly with lemon juice and paprika. Roll each oyster with a half-slice of bacon and slip it onto a skewer. Place skewers on well-greased grill, 4 to 6 inches above the hot coals. Cook until bacon is just cooked through — don't overcook the oysters. Serve on buttered toast, garnished with lemon slices and watercress. **Serves 6 as appetizer, 4 as first course.**

Cook's Tip: *Here are a few more ideas for oysters on skewers. Alternate oysters with ham and tiny red tomatoes. Or dip oysters in melted butter and alternate on skewers with mushrooms and green pepper strips. Brush with butter and broil 4 to 6 minutes, just until oysters are plump.*

Scampi on Skewers

½ cup olive oil
1 tsp. oregano
3 garlic cloves, minced
2 Tbsp. lemon or lime juice
¼ tsp. salt
2 pounds large shrimp, cleaned and shelled

Make marinade by combining first 5 ingredients. Slit shells of shrimp and remove vein, if desired. Place shrimp in flat dish; cover with marinade and refrigerate, covered, 3 to 4 hours.

Thread shrimp on 4 to 6 skewers and place on well-greased grill, 4 to 6 inches above the hot coals. Cook 15 to 20 minutes, turning and brushing occasionally with the garlic butter marinade. Serve hot. (You can vary this recipe by alternating the shrimp with tiny tomatoes, green pepper or onion slices. Or how about wrapping bacon strips around the cleaned raw shrimp? You may also remove lobster tails from their shells, cut the meat into chunks, and substitute it for the shrimp — eliminate the garlic, if you like.) **Serves 4 to 6.**

Florida Fish, Indian Style

(roasted in corn husks)

- 6 ears fresh Florida sweet corn, with husks on
- 6 1- to 1½-pound whole fish, pan dressed (bream, weakfish or small pompano)
- 1½ sticks butter
- 1 tsp. dried parsley flakes, crushed
- 1 clove garlic, minced
- 2 Tbsp. seasoned salt
- freshly ground pepper
- 6 tsp. lemon juice

Start fire and let it burn down to coals. Remove corn from husks and set it aside for later use. Strip silks from husks and soak husks in cold water 5 minutes. Cut butter into 2-tablespoon pieces and place inside cleaned, dressed fish. Scatter parsley flakes, minced garlic, salt, a grind of black pepper and one teaspoon lemon juice inside each fish. Wrap each fish in a corn husk and tie end with cord. Place fish in husks atop coals and cover with more coals. Cook about 15 minutes, or until fish flakes easily and is opaque. Serve one fish to each guest, with knife to cut cord. **Serves 6.**

Smoky Barbecued Fish Fillets

- 2 pounds drum, tilefish, grouper or other thick fish fillets
- 1 cup catsup, divided
- ⅓ cup lemon or lime juice
- ¼ vegetable oil
- 2 tsp. Worcestershire sauce
- ½ cup onion, chopped
- 1 tsp. sugar
- ¼ tsp. Tabasco sauce
- ¼ tsp. liquid smoke
- 1 bay leaf

Cut fish into serving-size portions. Place fish in single layer in shallow glass baking dish. Combine ½ cup catsup, lemon juice, oil, Worcestershire sauce and garlic. Pour sauce over fish. Cover and refrigerate one hour, turning fish once.

Remove fish and save sauce. To this sauce, add remaining catsup, onion, ¼ cup water, sugar, liquid Tabasco, liquid smoke and bay leaf. Simmer 20 minutes to thicken and blend flavors.

Place fish in well-oiled hinged wire basket and baste with sauce. Cook 5 inches above moderately hot coals 6 to 8 minutes. Baste with sauce and cook other side 8 minutes, or until fish flakes easily with a fork. Brush fish with sauce as needed during cooking. Serve with remaining marinade poured over fish. Many people like this with their favorite cold beer. **Serves 4 to 6.**

Swordfish in Mustard Sauce

2 cups clam juice
1 cup heavy cream
2 Tbsp. Dijon mustard with wine
6 8-oz. swordfish steaks, 1 inch thick
¼ cup butter, melted
¼ cup margarine, melted
2 Tbsp. thyme
freshly ground pepper
¼ cup parsley, minced

Start barbecue fire and allow to burn down to coals. Be sure grill is clean and well-oiled.

To make sauce, boil clam juice in saucepan until reduced by half. Add cream; cook until thick enough to coat a spoon. Add mustard and stir until well blended; turn heat low and keep warm. Don't let sauce boil.

Rinse fish in cold water and pat dry with paper towels. Brush fish with butters, mixed. Sprinkle with thyme. Place fish on grill about 5 inches above hot coals; cook, turning once and allowing 10 minutes of cooking time for each inch of steaks' thickness. Spoon sauce onto warmed plates. Top with fish. Sprinkle with parsley and freshly ground pepper. Serve immediately. **Serves 6.**

Beer-Battered Florida Trout (Weakfish)

(Key Largo could be the setting for this fish feast.)

1¼ cups packaged biscuit mix
¾ cup beer
1 egg
¼ tsp. salt
½ tsp. thyme
4 pan-dressed Florida weakfish
peanut oil

Beat together biscuit mix, beer, egg, salt and thyme. Rinse fish under cold water; drain and wipe dry with paper towels. Dip in batter to thoroughly coat all surfaces. Place oil in heavy frying pan over coals and heat until very hot. Fry fish in hot oil about 4 minutes; turn carefully and cook other side 3 to 4 minutes or until done. Serve with tartar sauce and Florida lime slices. **Serves 4.**

Zesty Grilled Spanish Mackerel

4 1-lb. Spanish mackerel fillets
¼ cup lemon juice
1 tsp. grated lemon rind
¼ cup French dressing
1 tsp. salt
½ tsp. pepper

Rinse fillets and pat them dry with paper towels. Combine remaining ingredients in glass dish; place fish in dish, cover and refrigerate 20 minutes. Start fire in grill; burn charcoal down to coals. Place fillets in well-oiled, hinged wire basket. Cook over moderately hot coals, 5 inches above heat, 5 to 7 inches on each side, depending on thickness of fish. Allow 10 minutes of cooking time for each inch thickness of fish. Great with potatoes baked in the coals. **Serves 4.**

Cook's Tip: *Natives of the Bahamas, where fish has always been a staple in the diet, usually cook their fish with the head left on, because they say that's where the sweetest meat lies.*

Smoking Fish and Seafood

Almost any fish can be smoked, as can lobster, shrimp and clams. Cook small fish whole and cut larger fish into fillets. Remove oily skins. Use Kosher salt for smoke cooking, because table salt contains chemical additives. Recipes given below are for hot smoking, which requires from 1 to 8 hours. Cold smoking of fish requires up to 36 hours and may continue for several days.

Smoked Oysters

24 medium oysters, in shells
¼ cup butter or margarine, melted
2 Tbsp. parsley, finely chopped
1 small garlic clove, minced
½ tsp. salt
⅛ tsp. freshly ground white pepper
2½ tsp. fresh lemon juice

On a regular covered grill, oysters cook in such a short time — about 10 minutes — that they don't have that smoky flavor, so you must cook them in a water smoker. Follow manufacturer's instructions for your smoker. Place oysters on grill; lower cover and smoke cook one hour. (Oysters will open as they cook.) Combine remaining ingredients, blending well. Guests may dip their oysters into the sauce. **Serves 6 as appetizer.**

Smoked Whole Mullet

6 1-pound whole mullet, cleaned
1 cup Kosher salt
1 gallon water
1 pound hickory chips
¼ cup vegetable oil

The night before cooking, soak hickory chips in 2 quarts of water. To smoke fish, use a charcoal fire in a barbecue grill with a hood or cover that closes to make a smoker. Start fire 30 minutes before cooking time, and let it burn down to glowing coals, half covered with ash.

Wash mullet inside and out in cold running water. Trim black membrane from stomach cavity. Remove head just below the collarbone. Cut along backbone almost to the tail; fish should lie flat in one piece.

Add salt to cold water and stir until dissolved. Place fish in glass dish, pour brine over them, and refrigerate for 30 minutes.

When ready to cook, squeeze most of the water from wood chips and sprinkle them on coals. Dip paper towel in vegetable oil and oil grill thoroughly. Close grill, leaving top and bottom vents open for about 5 minutes, to allow smoke to build up. Remove mullet from refrigerator; rinse well to remove salt. Pat dry with paper towels and rub with vegetable oil. Be sure skin side is well oiled. Place skin side down on oiled grill over smoking fire. Lower cover and smoke 1½ hours, adding wet chips every 15 minutes to keep fire smoking.

Increase temperature by adding more charcoal to fire and opening the draft. Brush fish sparingly with oil. Cover and cook 15 minutes. Brush fish again with oil and cook 10 minutes longer or until fish is lightly browned. **Serves 6.**

Smoke-Flavored Vegetables

Serve these with smoked fish and shellfish:

Onions Allow one onion for each person. Peel whole onions and rub lightly with vegetable oil. Place onions on grill and smoke cook for 1 to 1½ hours, depending on the hotness of the fire.

Potatoes Use either Irish potatoes or sweet potatoes. Scrub with a brush and rub skins with vegetable oil or melted butter. With a fork, punch several holes in each potato, then place on grill. Allow 2½ hours or more cooking time.

Sweet Corn Allow one ear for each person. Without removing corn, turn back husks and remove the silks. Spread corn thoroughly with melted butter; sprinkle with regular or seasoned salt. Pull husks back into place; secure ends with string. Smoke cook on grill for one hour and 15 minutes, or until corn is tender.

Eat These With Fish

Old Southern traditions persist in Florida. To many Floridians, it wouldn't be a fish fry without tasty, hot little hush puppies. Making hot breads with cornmeal dates back to Indian days.

While many folks choose French-fried potatoes, natives of the Old South serve old-fashioned grits with their fish dinners. And what Floridian doesn't delight in desserts made with the incomparable key lime!

Here are a few favorite traditional foods to serve with your Florida fish.

Sweet and Sour Cole Slaw

(Southern style)

1 large cabbage, cored, finely chopped
1 medium green pepper, finely chopped
1 small red pepper, finely chopped
1 medium sweet onion, finely chopped
1 cup sugar
1 tsp. salt
1 tsp. dry mustard
1 tsp. celery seed (or more)
1 cup vinegar
2/3 cup vegetable oil

Shred cabbage and combine with chopped peppers and onion; set aside. In saucepan, combine sugar, salt, mustard, celery seed and vinegar; bring to a boil. Stir until sugar dissolves. Remove from heat. Add oil and cool to room temperature. Pour marinade over cabbage mixture. Refrigerate overnight; serve well chilled. **Serves 6.**

Creamy Cole Slaw

(Northern style)

- 1 large cabbage, cored and finely chopped
- ½ cup green pepper, finely chopped
- 1 Tbsp. minced onion
- 1 tsp. celery seed
- 2 carrots, grated
- ½ tsp. salt
- 1 tsp. mustard
- 2 tsp. sugar
- dash cayenne pepper
- 2 Tbsp. all-purpose flour
- 1 egg, beaten slightly
- ¾ cup light cream
- ¼ cup vinegar

Shred cabbage. Add green pepper, onion, celery seed and carrots. Set aside. In top of double boiler (or over low heat in heavy saucepan), place salt, mustard, sugar and cayenne. Stir in flour, egg, cream, vinegar. Stir; cook over boiling water until slightly thick. Cool; refrigerate.

Combine well-chilled cream dressing with cabbage mixture. Refrigerate several hours; serve cold. (Note: A quick, easy dressing may be made by mixing mayonnaise with a little honey and lemon juice.) **Serves 6.**

French Fried Onion Rings

- 4 large mild sweet onions, thickly sliced
- ice water
- 1 cup all-purpose flour
- 1 tsp. salt
- 1 tsp. baking powder
- ¾ cup milk
- 1 egg yolk, slightly beaten
- 1 Tbsp. vegetable oil
- 1 egg white

Peel onions and slice ¼-inch wide. Separate into rings and soak in ice water 1 hour. Drain on paper towels and pat dry. Make batter by sifting together flour, salt and baking powder. Set aside. Beat egg white until soft but not dry. Beat egg yolk slightly, stir in milk and vegetable oil. Combine with flour mixture and stir until smoothly blended. Gently fold beaten egg white into batter.

Heat oil in deep fat fryer (or in deep, heavy frying pan) to 375°F. Dip onion rings into batter, shaking off drippings, and fry a few at a time until golden brown. Place in bowl lined with paper towels; cover and keep warm until all onions are fried. Sprinkle with salt and serve hot. (Note: This batter also works well with other fried foods such as zucchini or mushrooms.) **Serves 4 to 6.**

Hush Puppies

- 2 cups cornmeal
- 1 Tbsp. all-purpose flour
- 1 tsp. baking soda
- 1 tsp. baking powder
- 2 tsp. salt
- 1 cup buttermilk
- 1 egg, slightly beaten
- 1 onion, finely chopped
- vegetable oil

Combine dry ingredients; add buttermilk, egg, onion, stirring lightly. Heat oil in deep fat fryer to 370°F. Drop batter by tablespoon into hot oil. Fry a few at a time, turning once, for 3 minutes or until golden brown. Drain on paper towels and serve at once. **Serves 4.**

Conchy Joe's Cornbread

(A great favorite in Jensen Beach)

- 2 cups yellow cornmeal
- 2 cups all-purpose flour
- 2 Tbsp. baking powder
- 1 tsp. salt
- ¼ cup light maple syrup
- 2 large eggs, beaten slightly
- 2 cups milk
- ⅓ cup butter, melted
- ⅓ cup sour cream

Sift together the cornmeal, flour, baking powder and salt. Add maple syrup, eggs, milk, butter and sour cream. Beat at low speed until fairly smooth, a minute or two. Do not overbeat. Pour batter into a greased 9 x 13-inch pan and bake 15 to 20 minutes at 400°F. Makes a moist bread, with a fine texture that doesn't crumble. **Serves 12.**

Cheesy Grits

- 4 cups water
- ¾ tsp. salt
- 1 cup quick grits
- ½ cup butter or margarine (1 stick)
- 6 oz. cheddar cheese, grated
- 2 eggs
- water
- 1 cup cornflake crumbs or crushed potato chips

In saucepan, bring water and salt to boil. Stir in grits. Cook 6 minutes. Remove from heat; stir in butter and grated cheese. Beat eggs slightly and add water to make 1 cup. Stir into grits. Pour into oiled 1½ quart casserole. Top with crumbs or crushed chips. Bake at 350°F for 45 minutes or until well set. Let stand a few minutes, then serve hot. **Serves 6 to 8.**

Frozen Limeade Pie (or Tarts)

(It's fancy, and it's fast)

1 chocolate crumb pie crust
1 6-oz. can frozen Florida limeade or lemonade
1 pint vanilla ice cream, softened
few drops green food coloring
1 8-oz. package frozen whipped topping

Use a ready-made pie crust from the grocer or make your own favorite chocolate crust. Place limeade concentrate in large mixing bowl; beat 30 seconds. Gradually spoon in ice cream and blend. Fold in thawed whipped topping and add a few drops green color. (If using lemonade, use yellow color.)

Whip mixture until smooth. If necessary, freeze until mixture stiffens and will mound. Spoon into pie crust or tart shells. Freeze until firm. Leftovers (if any) should be kept frozen. Garnish with whipped cream and lime slices. **Serves 6.**

Florida Key Lime Pudding Cake

¾ cup sugar
¼ cup all-purpose flour
dash salt
3 Tbsp. butter or margarine, melted
¼ tsp. grated key lime peel
¼ cup key lime juice
3 egg yolks
1½ cups milk
3 egg whites

In medium bowl, combine sugar, flour and salt. Add melted butter, lime peel and lime juice. Stir until blended. Set aside. Separate eggs into two bowls, being careful not to get any yolk in the whites. Beat egg yolks and then add the milk, stirring with a wooden or plastic spoon; stir into lime mixture.

In glass or china bowl (not plastic), beat egg whites until stiff. Fold gently into lime mixture. Pour batter into greased 8 x 8 x 2-inch baking pan. Pour hot water into a large, shallow baking pan to one-inch depth. Set pan of pudding batter into the hot water. Bake in 350°F oven 40 minutes or until lightly browned. Serve warm or chilled, topped with whipped cream or softened vanilla ice cream. **Serves 6.**

Seafood Sauces

You can turn ordinary cooked fish into gourmet fare with the addition of these delicious, easy-to-make sauces.

Cocktail Sauce

½ cup chili sauce
⅓ cup catsup
2 Tbsp. prepared horseradish
2 Tbsp. lemon or lime juice
1 tsp. Worcestershire sauce
dash cayenne pepper

Combine all ingredients in small bowl and mix well. Cover and refrigerate for 3 hours or more. Serve in cocktail glass with cold boiled shrimp, crabmeat or lobster. **Makes 1 cup.**

Dilly Tartar Sauce

2 cups mayonnaise or cooked salad dressing
⅓ cup garlic dill pickle, finely chopped
1 Tbsp. lemon or lime juice
1 3-oz. jar capers, finely chopped
1 Tbsp. chopped parsley
1 Tbsp. grated onion

Combine all ingredients in small bowl and mix well. Cover and refrigerate for 3 hours or more. Serve well chilled with any hot or cold fish. **Makes 2 cups.**

Spanish Sauce for Fish

1 16-oz. can stewed tomatoes
1 clove garlic, minced
½ cup onion, finely chopped
½ cup canned tomato sauce
2 tsp. Worcestershire sauce (or more, to taste)
½ tsp. sugar
¼ tsp. oregano
2 Tbsp. parsley, chopped
1 tsp. salt
⅛ tsp. pepper
2 Tbsp. cornstarch
¼ cup cold water

Cook tomatoes, garlic and onion in covered saucepan over low heat about 20 minutes, until onion is tender. Stir in tomato sauce, Worcestershire, sugar, oregano, parsley, salt and pepper. Set aside.

In small bowl, stir together the cornstarch and water until smooth. Pour into tomato mixture. Heat to boil; reduce heat and simmer uncovered 15 minutes, stirring occasionally. Pour over broiled or steamed fish fillets, or use as a sauce when baking fish. **Makes about 1½ pints.**

Tartar Sauce

- 1½ cups mayonnaise or cooked salad dressing
- ¼ cup sweet pickle relish
- 1 Tbsp. pimiento, chopped
- 1 tsp. fresh parsley, finely chopped
- 1 Tbsp. onion, finely chopped
- 1 tsp. Dijon mustard

Thoroughly combine all ingredients in small bowl. Cover and refrigerate 3 hours or more. Serve well chilled with any hot or cold fish. **Makes 2 cups.**

Garlic Butter Dip

(For shrimp or lobster)

- ½ cup (1 stick) butter
- 2 cloves garlic, minced
- 1 Tbsp. lemon or lime juice
- dash liquid red hot sauce

Melt butter in small saucepan, and stir in garlic, lemon juice and hot sauce. Cook 2 minutes, stirring occasionally. Pour into server while hot and invite guests to dip their cooked shrimp or lobster chunks. **Makes ½ cup.**

Basic White Sauce with Variations

(Bechamel Sauce)

- 2 Tbsp. butter
- 2 Tbsp. flour
- 1 cup milk or Half-and-Half
- ½ tsp. salt
- dash white pepper
- dash paprika

Melt butter in top of double boiler, over boiling water. Add flour, salt, pepper and paprika and stir until well blended. Gradually add milk, stirring constantly until sauce is thickened and smooth. Cook, stirring occasionally, 15 minutes. Serve hot.

Variations

Just before serving sauce, add one of the following:

Anchovy Sauce — Add 1 teaspoon anchovy paste and 2 tablespoons minced celery.

Cheese Sauce — Add ½ cup grated Cheddar or Swiss cheese, with ⅛ teaspoon dry mustard.

Cucumber Sauce — Add ½ cup chopped cucumber and 1 tablespoon chopped chives.

Newburg — Add 1 cup cooked or canned lobster meat and 2 tablespoons cream mixed with 1 beaten egg yolk.

More Variations

Onion Sauce — Add ¼ cup minced onion and ½ cup sour cream.

Mushroom Sauce — To one cup of White Sauce, add 1 3-oz. can sliced mushrooms (or ½ cup fresh chopped mushrooms). Beat 1 egg well; stir in ¼ cup of sauce. Mix with rest of the sauce and cook, stirring, over low heat, until slightly thick, about 2 minutes. Stir in 3 tablespoons sherry. Serve at once or keep warm over hot water.

Note: Any of the sauces above may be used in creamed or scalloped seafood dishes.

Savory Butters

Hot butter sauces are superb with many fish dishes such as broiled fish, boiled shrimp or lobster. Before starting a recipe, it's wise to clarify your butter. Why? Because clarified butter will not burn as easily, and it makes a more attractive-looking sauce.

How to Clarify Butter

Place 1 pound or less of unsalted butter in a saucepan. Over low heat, melt butter. A white substance will rise to the surface. Skim this off. Butter will clear and white sediment will sink to the bottom. Have ready several thicknesses of dampened cheesecloth. Strain butter through this and store in a covered jar until ready to use. It will keep indefinitely in the refrigerator. This simple butter, heated, is the drawn butter on seafood menus.

Flavored Butters

You can have a flavored butter ready when you need it by shaping the mixture into small balls, freezing on a cookie sheet, then placing in a freezer bag to be stored until needed.

Caviar Butter — To ¼ pound of butter, add 2 tablespoons red caviar (well crushed), and cream until smooth. Add a squeeze of lemon or lime juice, and ⅛ teaspoon pepper.

Beurre Meuniere In heavy frying pan, heat clarified butter steadily until it turns light toast brown. To ¼ pound of the butter, add 2 teaspoons chopped parsley and 1 teaspoon lemon juice. Immediately pour hot sauce over trout, salmon or other delicate cooked fish.

Dill Butter In blender or with hand whip, cream ¼ pound butter until light and fluffy. Blend in 4 tablespoons chopped dill, ¼ teaspoon salt and ½ tablespoon lemon or lime juice.

Herb Butter In a bowl, combine ¼ pound butter, 1 tablespoon fresh chopped parsley, 1 tablespoon finely chopped tarragon and 1 tablespoon chopped chives. Cream together until smooth; serve well chilled with hot fish dishes.

Lemon Butter

4 Tbsp. butter or margarine
1 Tbsp. lemon juice
1 tsp. grated lemon peel
1 Tbsp. parsley, chopped
½ tsp. salt
dash cayenne pepper

To serve hot, melt butter and add other ingredients. Serve hot over baked or broiled fish. To serve cold, cream butter until light and fluffy, then add other ingredients.

Variations

Mustard Butter To basic recipe, add 2 tablespoons Dijon mustard and 1 teaspoon chopped chives.

Whipped Cream Butter Prepare hot Lemon Butter; cool. Whip ¼ cup heavy cream and stir in. Chill.

Index

T